BLESSINGS
IN
BLOGS:
Living
Effectively

BLESSINGS IN BLOGS: Living Effectively

50 Bible-based Life Applications

GENIA M. OWENS

Order this book online at www.trafford.com
or email orders@trafford.com

Most Trafford titles are also available at major online book retailers.

Unless otherwise indicated, all Scripture quotations are from the King James Version (KJV) of the Holy Bible, originally published in 1611 under a patent secured by the British Crown. The copyright for the KJV is now regarded as public domain in most of the world outside the UK.

Brackets in Scripture quotations indicate in part descriptions from the author and Read-Along Translations from the King James Version, 1976, Thomas Nelson, Inc. Nashville, Tennessee. All rights reserved. Used by permission.

Reprinted by permission. Let The Journey Begin: God's Roadmap For New Beginnings, Max Lucado, 1998, Thomas Nelson, Inc. Nashville, Tennessee. All rights reserved.

"Behold the Beauty of Unity: Sermon Segment Two," Elder William R. Thicklin, July 2011, Family of Faith Ministries™, www.fofm.us/sermon.html (accessed July 14, 2011). Used by permission.

"What the Bible Says About Who and What We Are in Christ Jesus," Ephesians Chapter One, Midweek Bible Study, Reverend Michael E. Woods, August 31, 2011. Used by permission.

Excerpt from the Holman Bible Dictionary © 1991 Holman Bible Publishers. Used by permission.
Printed in the United States of America.

ISBN: 978-1-4669-1160-4 (sc)
ISBN: 978-1-4669-1159-8 (hc)
ISBN: 978-1-4669-1158-1 (e)

Library of Congress Control Number: 2012900778

Trafford rev. 02/22/2012

 www.trafford.com

North America & international
toll-free: 1 888 232 4444 (USA & Canada)
phone: 250 383 6864 ♦ fax: 812 355 4082

DEDICATIONS

This book is dedicated first to God my Heavenly Father, Jesus Christ my Lord and Savior, and the Holy Spirit who lives within me. *"Thine, O Lord, is the greatness, and the power, and the glory, and the victory, and the majesty: for all that is in the heaven and in the earth is thine; thine is the kingdom, O Lord, and thou art exalted as head above all"* (1 Chronicles 29:11).

❖ To my husband Roy C. Owens, whom I love dearly; and to our four gifts from God—Royce (our son), Erinn (our daughter), Lance* (our infant son), and Tyler* (our unborn child)—each of whom holds a very special place in my heart. *"Every good gift and every perfect gift is from above..."* (James 1:17a).

❖ To my grandmother Osceola* Furze.

❖ To my parents Barbara* and Eugene* Baskin; and my sisters and brothers-in-law: Fayetta and Ron Thicklin, Parys and Anthony Hall, Tina and Michael Woods, Viola and Terence Richardson, and Anita Wright; Donnie (Mitchell) Young, and Walter Wright, II.

❖ To my maternal aunts and uncles: Dolores* and Ben* Williams; Annette* and James* Bell.

❖ To my cousins Bernard* and Arthur* Bentley and their families; Fabian,* Ben, and Rod Williams, and Jetta (Williams) Jones and her family; Scott and Akilah Smith and their children Mikalah, Micah, and Miah.

❖ To my parents-in-law Hattie and Roy B.* Owens; and my sisters-and brothers-in-law: Karen* Lewis, Sherry Smith and Esosa Osawaru, Cozetta and Marvin Williams, Veda and Stacy Holmes,

Irene Green, Ron and Don Owens, and Patricia and Willie Felton; Ricky* Smith, Terry Green, and Teresa Owens.

❖ To my aunts- and uncles-in-law Mary* Baker, Josephine Sims, Connie, Charles*, and Danny Alexander, and Corrine* Anderson.

❖ To my cousins-in-law Ricky Jordan, Greg Baker, and Penny Anderson.

❖ To my nieces and nephews: Kimberly Young and Melvin Brooks; Parys A., Victoria (daughter: Chloe), Anthony II, and Victor Hall; Christina and Jonathan Long (children: Amarah, Malcolm, and Jordyn), Jana and Randiele Henderson (son: Donte), and Lori Woods; Keith and Alex Richardson; Walter III and Daniel Wright; Cher-Ron Thicklin (children: William *aka Diamond*, Sean, Donovan, and Yiternatee *aka Sugar*); Tanisha and Willie Garfield (children: Xavier, Niona, and Kiara), and Takiesha Watson; Shelby (children: Sophia and Cassius), Jacqueline, and Janae Smith; Marcia (children: Jason and Quinn), Chandler, Kyle, Taylor, and Chelsea Williams; BreAnna, Brandess, Brittney, and Bryson Holmes; Azariah and Solomon Green; Jahia and Nailah Owens; Sidra, Ember, and Harper Felton.

❖ Also, to family members not listed, and those who are yet to come.

May this dedication bless and keep us united as a family in Christ.

*In loving memory.

CONTENTS

LIST OF ILLUSTRATIONS

COVER

After the Rain, by Roy C. Owens, GREO Galleries Unlimited™, Tyler Gallery (www.greoart.com)

THREE STAGE MODEL

"Using the Upside of the Brain" developed and designed by Genia M. Owens

PHOTOS ON FIRST PAGE OF EACH BLOG

Reprinted by permission. Images are photographed by Genia M., Roy C., Royce A., and Erinn K. Owens—thus, forming the company name, GREO Galleries Unlimited™ *(with the two "Rs" as one)*—www.greoart.com. Copyright © 2007 – 2011. All rights reserved. *(Images printed in this book are black and white cropped sections of the original GREO photos. They are listed below by blog date, blog title, GREO website gallery, title of photo, and photographer. PreGallery indicates GREO photos not on display in a GREO website gallery).* View the full images and the entire collection of GREO Galleries Unlimited™ at www.greoart.com.

SUMMER SECTION

June 1, Using the Upside of the Brain, Kyndal: *Possibilities,* Genia M. Owens (gmo)

June 3, Never a Dull Moment, Tyler: *What Now,* Roy C. Owens (rco)

June 7, The Greatest Investment, PreGallery: *SOS2:1,* gmo

June 18, I Believe That Was Yesterday, VanRoss: *Bold Beauty,* gmo

June 24, What Did You Learn? Royce: *Houston2,* Royce A. Owens (rao)

July 4, Live Like We Are Saved, Tyler: *Palm Tree,* gmo

January 25, Sisters, Mizel: *Princess 1,* gmo

February 5, Saved for a Purpose, Marie: *At the Beach 1,* Erinn K. Owens (eko)

February 14, God's Love is Forever, Marie: *White Blossoms,* rco

February 22, Two Birds, PreGallery: *Two Birds,* gmo, eko

SPRING SECTION

March 1, What's in a Moment? Tyler: *One Moment,* gmo

March 12, About Tithing, Marie: *Faith,* rco

March 29, Why Aren't We There Yet?, Calvin: *Destiny,* gmo

April 2, While We Wait, Lance: *Tomorrow,* rao

April 6, Together As One, PreGallery: *As One,* gmo

April 7, God Answers Prayer, Calvin: *Amazing,* gmo

April 9, When God Calls, Listen, Kyndal: *Midnight Blue,* rco

April 10, There's Something About Water, Calvin: *The Falls,* rco

April 13, What Do You See? Tyler: *Behold,* rco

May 3, Follow God's Perfect Plan, PreGallery: *Sky,* gmo

May 14, Praise the Lord, Kyndal: *Rocky Road,* rco

May 18, Action Speaks Louder with the Word, Calvin: *Rushing,* rao

May 21, Blog Bites, Tyler: *Bonnets,* rco

May 30, Able to Stand, Calvin: *Galleria Trees,* gmo

ACKNOWLEDGEMENTS

To all who supported me in this endeavor or made a significant impact in my life.

❖ **Roy C. Owens, my husband.** Thank you for your love, prayers and support by listening to excerpts of my book and giving feedback throughout the writing process. Thank you also for taking an author photo of me and many beautiful GREO images over the years that amazingly illustrate my book. For the wonderful person that you are and all that you do, I love you completely.

❖ **Royce A. and Erinn K. Owens, our son and daughter.** Thank you for making my life rich with moments to cherish forever. Also, for listening to excerpts of the book and sharing your GREO photos for the interior. I love you both dearly.

❖ **My five beautiful sisters: four who reviewed sections of the manuscript and provided valuable feedback; and one who inspired me to pursue my interest in writing.** I thank God for each of you. I am blessed tremendously with five amazing role models.

Fayetta L. Thicklin. Bachelor of Arts in Elementary Education, Master of Science in Education Administration; Elementary School Principal in the Midwest. You have demonstrated a true passion for education through years of experience as a teacher and principal. I truly appreciate the time and effort you spent supporting me in this endeavor.

Parys L. K. Hall. Bachelor of General Studies in Business Administration and Accounting, Master of Information Systems Management, and Master of Project Management. Your ability to understand the scope of a project was very instrumental in the layout of the first section and in your suggestion that I design a model to illustrate the concept of "Using the Upside of the Brain."

Tina E. Woods. Bachelor of Business Administration in Accounting; Accountant. Your analytical experience contributed significantly to your thorough review of my manuscript. I am truly grateful for the support you have shown in all my endeavors, including purchasing a print from the online art gallery my husband and I established (GREO Galleries Unlimited™, www. greoart.com).

Viola M. Richardson. Bachelor of Science in Social Science; Real Estate Broker, Owner of Mizel Real Estate Inv. Grp. LLC, Founder of Family of Faith Ministries™ (FoFM™—www.fofm. us). You are truly committed to supporting each of us in our endeavors—especially reviewing the first draft of my manuscript while on vacation overseas. Thank you for the sacrifice, and for writing the Foreword, including words of kindness and a beautiful story about our aunt. Thank you also for purchasing prints from my online art gallery.

Anita R. Wright. Your writing abilities and creative illustration of the series you wrote for our family newsletter *(The FAM™— Family Articles Monthly, 1994-1995)* contributed to my interest in writing. Thank you for the inspiration.

❖ **Kimberly C. Young.** Bachelor of Arts in Public Policy Studies, Master of Business Administration, and Master of Management in Hospitality; Executive Director. As my first-born niece, you are a beautiful, professional young woman and a role model for your cousins. I am very proud of you. May God continue to bless and keep you always.

❖ **My brothers-in-law who were supportive in this endeavor.**

Elder William R. Thicklin. Your words of inspiration shared through your sermons on the Family of Faith Ministries™ website are encouragement to the heart, food for the soul, and evidence of your love for God and your family. Thank you for allowing me to include one of your quotes in my book.

Reverend Michael E. Woods. Your love and commitment to God is clearly demonstrated through your sermons, directing the choir, and your love for your family. I am very grateful that you allowed me to include one of your quotes as well.

Terence Richardson. You are a prime example of how *with God, all things are possible.* Your faith in God is evident in your life, family, profession, and the many lives you touch. Words cannot describe how supportive you have been over the years including high school and college days. Thank you for reviewing the content of the book cover.

❖ **Cheri Winne.** The hundred percent that you give as a teacher who genuinely cares about her students is the reason I am truly thankful for your support in editing a draft of my manuscript. Your feedback is greatly appreciated and your comments are very encouraging.

❖ **Janet Hendrix.** Words cannot express how you have made this endeavor worth every effort. Thank you from the bottom of my heart for taking the time to edit a draft of my manuscript and provide encouraging feedback. I pray that God will continue to bless you as you have blessed me.

❖ **Rev. Charles B. Bailey and Mrs. Geneva Bailey, Kansas City, KS.** As faithful followers of Christ, you will always be an inspiration to all who are blessed to have known you. I am very grateful for Rev. Bailey's pastoral leadership and Mrs. Bailey's passion for Christian Education during my childhood as a member of Salem Baptist Church. May your legacy live forever through the many lives you have touched and through the Bailey Christian Education Fund (BCEF) Scholarship (www.cbbailey.com).

❖ **Pastors Joe and Lori Champion, Senior Pastors, Georgetown, TX.** God has truly blessed Pastor Joe with the gift of teaching and preaching, and with a vision to impact millions of lives; and Pastor Lori (an inspiration to all women of faith) with the gift of encouragement through speaking and singing. Through Christ, you both make an amazing difference worldwide. I am blessed by your faithfulness to God.

❖ **Pastor Wade Sutherland, Family Pastor, Georgetown, TX.** Thank you for your theological review of one of the most significant yet debated subjects of my book—*tithing*. Your support is truly a blessing and greatly appreciated.

❖ **Rev. Dr. Dave Koppel, Senior Pastor, Round Rock, TX.** Thank you for reviewing my manuscript and also providing theological insight. Your feedback laid the ground for meaningful discussion as this book reaches the hands of individuals from all backgrounds, cultures, and religions.

- ❖ **Veda Monday.** Thank you for being a true inspiration through your innovative methods for youth Bible study. As a ministry leader, you taught me to not only memorize Scriptures, but also to apply their Biblical principles to my life, which is the basis behind my book.

- ❖ **Harriet Bigham.** Thank you for being such an inspiring art teacher during my high school years. You brought out the creativity in me and helped me see life from a different perspective. I truly appreciate the artistic opportunities you always introduced to the class.

- ❖ **Lance Kivell.** Owner of Austin Network Services, Inc, Georgetown, TX. By taking the time to clearly communicate technical detail, you have inspired me to take courses in technology to expand my skill set. Thank you for making customer care as important as the full range of computer network services your company provides (www.austinns.com).

- ❖ **Andrew Frascone** (www.northaustinweb.com). Thank you for such a quick response in providing an educational resource for my web development studies that will help prepare me for designing and maintaining a website for my book. Your support is a reflection of the quality of service you provide.

- ❖ **Everyone who has made a positive impact in my life.** Thank you for surrounding me with encouragement and prayers.

FOREWORD

"The Bible clearly shows us that
God wants us to be prosperous in every area of life.
That is why He blessed us not only with His Word
but also with the spirit-filled words of other
Christian men and women."
~~ VMR

"Christianity, in its purest form,
is nothing more than seeing Jesus."
"Christian service, in its purest form,
is nothing more than imitating him who we see."
"To see his Majesty and to imitate him,
that is the sum of Christianity."
~~ Max Lucado

IN WRITING THE Foreword for BLESSINGS IN BLOGS: Living Effectively, I would like to express how the writings of Christian authors can touch the lives of others. For years I have been inspired by Max Lucado, my absolute favorite author among many authors. He has a way of making written words come alive. I remember visiting my beloved aunt in the hospital, right before she went home to be with the Lord. It was in the middle of winter and very cold. The streets were messy and all of nature seemed to be in a deep sleep.

As I stood in intensive care beside her bed, I could see the life being drained from her. I could tell she was struggling to let me know she wasn't going to give up. She appeared so small and weak and was very much dependent on every tube that proceeded to come from her body.

I recall how I drew strength from her eyes as I stood beside her bed. I could see life from within her eyes and it was then that I began to read several passages from Max Lucado's book, Let the Journey Begin—God's Roadmap for New Beginnings. This book was so fitting for such a difficult time, and it was out of sheer determination of wanting her to stay with me a little longer that I continued to read well into the night. I knew she could hear every word I was saying and each passage carried its own weight as it ministered to me and my aunt.

Of course there are quite a few talented and spirit-filled authors in the industry, authors who have the gift to minister to others who are hurting. But, just as I was blessed by the writings of Max Lucado, I have been blessed once again by the writings of another spirit-filled author, Genia Owens. Yes, once again, I can feel God's hand moving throughout each page of this well written creation.

I first became aware of Genia Owens' style of writing through a monthly newsletter she developed for a local church. Her writing was fresh, creative, and very informative. Next, I witnessed her writing style through a Christian-based website, Family of Faith Ministries™ (FoFM™). She is the website developer for FoFM™ and much of her God-given talents are shown throughout the website. It is so amazing to see the precious light of God's Word incorporated throughout her work; and through Jesus Christ our Lord and Savior, she has written a beautiful gift—BLESSINGS IN BLOGS: Living Effectively.

Her book truly invites each reader to search their heart while they read the subjects she has written. She provides the reader with a unique perspective, by posing such questions as **"What's in a Moment"** or **"Why Aren't We There Yet?"** As you follow along, you begin to sense that she has walked in your shoes, and that she can empathize with you in any given situation.

In a very subtle way, Genia Owens has invoked a touch of humor within her topics. For example, **"People, Read Your Bible!"** How ingenious is that, to take a familiar topic and add a twist to it, all the while conveying her message. She writes in terms that are plain and simple, yet she has a way of reminding us to take the time to read God's Word daily because **"Action Speaks Louder with the Word."**

We all have days when we feel hopeless with many insurmountable and daunting tasks we face. While facing these day to day hardships, sometimes our faith becomes shaken. When this happens, we want to limit God or *place Him in a box*. That is when reading the blogs can bless us with a different perspective, letting us know how God can remove the box. They address everyday situations making us aware that even with our limited abilities there is a resourceful God that has no limits.

Written by Viola Richardson

PREFACE

BLESSINGS IN BLOGS: Living Effectively is an inspirational message to all who are saved[5] by the grace of our Lord Jesus Christ, Son of the Living God. Through the representation of real and fictional characters, this book seeks to shed light on everyday situations, so we as Christians may respond more effectively in Christ and glorify God in Heaven. Likewise, it demonstrates to the unsaved[7] the blessings of belonging to the Savior. Through fifty Bible-based life applications, the blessings in the blogs are peace, joy, love, and a greater passion for the Word of God.

From inspiration to the production of this book I have experienced how God orchestrates what He has purposed through the content, format, input, prayers, and publisher. Even the title of the book reflects how God is in complete control of every detail in that the acronym of the title spells the word *BIBLE*, God's Holy Word. The Bible says in Ecclesiastes 7:1, *"A good name is better than precious ointment . . ."* It sets apart and defines purpose. Thus, the title was selected as a reminder that no matter what we face in life, we are blessed with a purpose that God will fulfill in and through us as we focus on His Word and follow Christ. This blessed endeavor is a reminder that *". . . all things work together for good to them that love God, to them who are the called according to his purpose"* (Romans 8:28). With this in mind, I truly believe that everything happens for a reason and every purpose designed by God will be fulfilled according to His plan.

Just over a year ago I started writing Bible-based blogs that I originally intended to post on a website I wanted to design and develop. Instead, God inspired me to combine the blogs as chapters of a book so they will be readily available without Internet access. Essentially, He gave me the opportunity to reach others with a physical format to encourage Bible study and application for spiritual growth.

While referencing God's Holy Word, my eyes were opened to see life from a new perspective. Now as I share my thoughts, experiences, and observations, I appreciate the inspiring words of the Psalmist who wrote, *"Thy word is a lamp unto my feet, and a light unto my path"* (Psalm 119:105). Jesus is the Word (John 1:1) and the Light who directs our paths. He said, *". . . I am the light of the world: he that followeth me shall not walk in darkness, but shall have the light of the life"* (John 8:12). God allows us to see more clearly when we follow *the Light.*

Writing BLESSINGS IN BLOGS: Living Effectively required not only inspirational content, but also a structure that reflects the typical features of a blog posted on the Internet. Most blogs are posted as often as monthly, weekly, or several times a day. The date, time, title, and thoughts are essential elements of a *blog*, which is simply defined as a *Web log. Bloggers* generally write about subjects that are very informative or creative—basically something they would like to share with the world: to educate or express an opinion, to encourage or entertain, to inform or make a difference.

As I present each blog in the form of a chapter, I pray that you will follow along with your Bible to see the correlation between situations of Biblical times and situations of modern days. The Bible contains true stories about people that lived during Biblical times and the situations they faced. These stories in general illustrate some of the same situations we face today, but in a very different setting. To fully understand how God's principles apply to today we must be willing to let down our guard, dismiss our first impression, and put away our opinions and expectations. Then we will receive the Light of *Truth* (John 17:17) and God will wipe away any doubt or confusion (1 Corinthians 14:33) that tries to hinder spiritual growth. To emphasize how Scriptures can apply to various situations, certain Scriptures are repeated throughout the book.

Similar to entries of a diary, blogs are usually published in reverse chronological order on a webpage, whereby the most current entry is at the top of the page. Alternatively, the entries printed in this book are presented in chronological order and divided into four seasonal sections: Summer, Fall, Winter, and Spring. Each seasonal section contains the months recognized by the Northern Hemisphere: Summer blogs written in June, July, and August; Fall blogs written in September, October, and November; Winter blogs written in December, January, and February; and Spring blogs written in March, April, and May.

The more I thought about this layout, the more I noticed an interesting correlation between the four seasons of the year and the spiritual seasons of life represented in the Bible, which was instrumental in determining the order of each section. The Bible provides an amazing account of life experiences starting with "The Creation" recorded in the book of Genesis and ending with "The Last Days," recorded in the book of Revelation. Thus, the order of the seasonal sections in BLESSINGS IN BLOGS: Living Effectively is inspired by what I believe is the order of the most recognized events that occurred in the Bible—even though the *content* of each blog is unrelated to the seasons.

The first seasonal section of the book is titled "Summer" because this vibrant and colorful season reflects the beauty of the Garden of Eden mentioned in Genesis—the first book of the Bible. The next section is titled "Fall," signifying the fall of humanity[3] as a result of sin—*what separates us from God* (Isaiah 59:2). "Winter" follows, representing what we sometimes see as a bitter struggle while we learn to submit to God's will. "Spring," is the final section which I associate with the fulfillment of God's promise that we can receive a new life in Christ Jesus.

The first blog introduces a technique I refer to as "Using the Upside of the Brain." It defines and demonstrates the technique using a model to illustrate the process as it relates to God's Word. Though not represented in every blog, this technique is the underlying thread of inspiration throughout the entire book to emphasize the importance of studying and applying God's Word. While writing this book I found several opportunities to practice "Using the Upside of the Brain."

The final feature of this book is the additional space for comments. Writing comments is one of the most essential features of a blog because it allows readers to reflect on what was read and express their thoughts. On the Internet, comments promote interaction, allowing visitors to not only record their input but also receive insight from the comments of others. To share your comments in response to the blogs printed in this book, I encourage you to participate in, or form, a discussion group or book club. You may also visit my website at www.2edify.us. *"Let us therefore follow after the things which make for peace, and things wherewith one may edify[2] another"* (Romans 14:19).

This book references the King James Version (KJV) of the Holy Bible. The KJV is an older version that I love to read because of its rich historical and poetic presence. Though the KJV provides an incredible learning experience, I encourage you to study with the Bible translation of your choice for optimal understanding. *"Wisdom is the principal thing; therefore get wisdom: and with all thy getting get understanding"* (Proverbs 4:7).

The more we understand, the more we will live effectively through Christ Jesus for the glory of God.

"Living effectively is not whether
God lifts us up out of our situations,
but whether we lift God up
by our faith in Him."
~~ *Genia*

SUMMER SECTION

"Using the Upside of the Brain"

Life was never intended to follow what seems fair or right by our plans. As we reach for the life we envision, we may experience situations that we do not understand. Yet, if we keep our eyes on Jesus and allow the Holy Spirit to lead, we are blessed with the peace God promised (John 14:27) that enables us to fulfill the purpose He called us to achieve.

Situations, no matter how great or small, will invariably catch us off guard and cause us to react according to how we think or feel. They can leave us disappointed, defensive, or doubtful—lacking confidence in God's power to help us overcome adversity. Our initial response reveals whether we allow the Holy Spirit to direct us with the Truth, or whether we respond based on how the situation seems. In other words, will we choose to respond spiritually by applying God's Word or naturally through our sinful nature (Galatians 5:17). A natural response may be triggered by logic or emotions, sometimes evoking doubt or confusion and keeping us from moving forward according to God's plan. Alternatively, a spiritual response allows us to be more productive and realize our purpose by studying God's Word—*Biblical instructions He has provided for effective living.*

At times we choose not to follow instructions. We anxiously seek the quickest solution and try to figure things out on our own. Therefore, we really cannot expect to benefit from our efforts if we are not willing to do what is required for optimal results. If we do not take time to study the Word of God regularly, we cannot expect to grow *". . . in the knowledge of our Lord and Saviour Jesus Christ"* (2 Peter 3:18). By studying God's Word we respond to our situations with spiritual truth rather than natural impulse. Even though we are naturally inclined to see life from our own perspective, we must **not** depend solely on logic or emotions.

For instance, when facing uncertainty, a situation that we do not understand, we automatically turn to logic because we naturally seek an explanation for everything. However, logic requires sound judgment, and none of the participants in a situation are able to see its fullness from the perfect perspective of God. He is omnipresent (*everywhere*-Ps. 139:7-10), omniscient (*all-knowing*-Isa. 40:13), and omnipotent (*almighty*-Gen. 17:1; Jn 1:3). Without God, human logic alone produces an incomplete source of reference, resulting in an ungodly response. Rather than lean on our own understanding, we should trust God (Proverbs 3:5) and know that some situations occur because God has a purpose greater than what we initially perceive. He knows what He is doing and certainly has the power and authority to achieve the results He desires. *"¹⁷Ah Lord God! behold, thou hast made the heaven and the earth by thy great power and stretched out arm, and there is nothing too hard for thee:" for "¹⁸ . . . the Great, the Mighty God, the Lord of hosts, is his name"* (Jeremiah 32:17,18b). Whether the results are immediate or in the years to come, we must keep our focus on God because He is faithful to fulfill His promises, allowing us to fulfill His plan no matter what we face.

Just as we tend to depend on logic, we sometimes turn to an emotional response based on our opinions or past experiences. When our eyes are fixed on how a situation *seems,* our response is affected by how we *feel.* Therefore, we tend to personalize the situation rather than view it from a *spiritual perspective*—that which reveals truth. An approach based solely on logic or emotions may be misleading. However, an approach based on allowing the Holy Spirit to lead will result in an effective response that glorifies God. How can we allow the Holy Spirit to lead? The model on page four demonstrates a simple and effective method I refer to as "Using the Upside of the Brain." It outlines the steps we go through when we choose to look up from our situations and allow the Holy Spirit to lead us.

For years, scientists explored how certain human attributes dominated by logic or emotions tend to be processed by a particular side of the human brain—left or right, though other studies may challenge the reliability of such findings. Nevertheless, rather than submitting to the logical (left) or emotional (right) side of the brain, the method of "Using the Upside of the Brain" allows us to see, understand, and respond to *what is really happening* in any situation without focusing on *assumptions or prideful expectations*. Based on Colossians 3:2, John 14:26 and Romans 12:2, this model is comprised of a simple three-step technique: (1) **refocus** on Christ, (2) **remember** God's Word, and (3) **renew** your mind. The purpose of this model is to demonstrate how to turn any uncertainty or adversity into an opportunity to glorify God. *"I will praise thee, O Lord my God, with all my heart: and I will glorify thy name for evermore"* (Psalm 86:12). With the help of the Holy Spirit the three steps point us in the right direction as we become confident in following Christ. The more confident we are *in Christ* (1 John 5:14) the better we are able to handle our situations more effectively.

The arrow in this model indicates an upward direction for upright living. It illustrates the significance of the *"upside"* of life, representing the benefits of living by the Word of God. "Using the Upside of the Brain" is not about reaching perfection, but rather living effectively for Christ and ultimately glorifying God.

"Using the Upside of the Brain"

Look up from your situation to glorify God
by responding more effectively in Christ

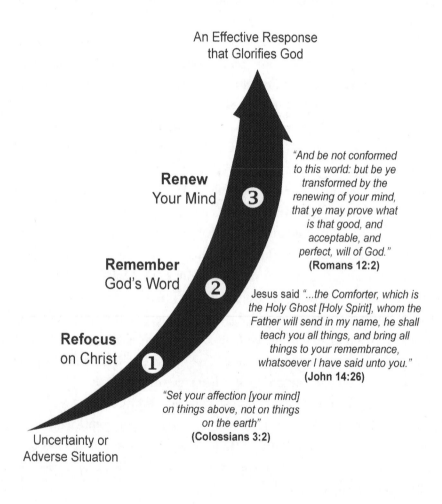

An Effective Response
that Glorifies God

Renew
Your Mind ③

*"And be not conformed
to this world: but be ye
transformed by the
renewing of your mind,
that ye may prove what
is that good, and
acceptable, and
perfect, will of God."*
(Romans 12:2)

Remember
God's Word ②

Jesus said *"...the Comforter, which is
the Holy Ghost [Holy Spirit], whom the
Father will send in my name, he shall
teach you all things, and bring all
things to your remembrance,
whatsoever I have said unto you."*
(John 14:26)

Refocus
on Christ ①

*"Set your affection [your mind]
on things above, not on things
on the earth"*
(Colossians 3:2)

Uncertainty or
Adverse Situation

An effective life in Christ is not a life that has never sinned, *"for all have sinned and come short of the glory of God* (Romans 3:23). Though not perfect, we seek to be like Christ Who is the only perfect example that we can follow. Christ represents the perfect way to live in harmony with others no matter what we face. Jesus' teachings, sacrifice, everlasting love, and Deity (John 17:5) have made an incredible impact on many lives over the years and will continue for generations to come. By focusing on what The Father sent Him to Earth to fulfill (John 20:21; John 10:10), Christ remains the perfect example of how we must commit to the will of God in order to accomplish His plans successfully. Through Christ's love and sacrifice, we are perfected (improved) (1 Peter 5:10; Hebrews 10:14; Hebrews 12:23; Matthew 5:48). *"Therefore if any man be in Christ, he is a new creature: old things are passed away; behold, all things are become new"* (2 Corinthians 5:17). When we accept Christ as our Lord and Savior we are no longer the same because our lives are no longer dictated by the things of this world. Instead, we are destined to live a life that is pleasing to God—a life filled with purpose. The life Christ lived while He was on Earth (based on unconditional love) is the perfect example of how we can have victory over any situation.

Thousands of years ago Christ demonstrated how to look up from a situation and focus on the will of God. Enduring tremendous pain and suffering, Christ stayed focused on the purpose for which He was sent—to save the world from eternal death. Despised, whipped, humiliated, and accused for no fault of His own, Christ could have responded defensively and fought back—forfeiting His purpose and the gift of eternal life for future generations. Yet He never allowed the situation to distract Him. Instead, He remained focused to achieve a greater purpose that made a lasting impact on the world.

He knew that the malicious act of violence against Him was not about Him personally as a man. It was about the human tendency to destroy what they (His accusers) did not understand. They chose not to believe that Jesus was the Messiah, fully man yet fully God (Philippians 2:5-8) because of their selfish-pride and fear of losing the power they thought they had achieved. Regardless of what appeared to be a devastating situation, Christ remained focused on God our Heavenly Father and the purpose God sent Him to Earth to fulfill. Though His crucifixion, a horrific act of violence, was intended to end His ministry, His loving sacrifice on the cross created a new life for all who choose to accept His priceless gift of salvation.

Now consider this: since Christ loves us enough to endure such an extreme situation, we are more than capable to look beyond our situations and focus on Christ as our example. We must *not* conform to the ways of this world by looking to the left or to the right because our ultimate goal is to respond in a manner that is pleasing to God (Philippians 2:13). We must allow the Holy Spirit to transform our hearts and our minds to immediately respond to the challenges of life in a Christ-like manner so that *". . . God in all things may be glorified through Jesus Christ . . ."* (1 Peter 4:11). By having confidence in Christ, we glorify God.

Remember, God has a specific purpose for each of us that He wants us to accomplish successfully. We cannot begin to imagine all that God can do in and through our lives. In fact, the Apostle Paul reminds us of God's wisdom when he said, *". . . Eye hath not seen, nor ear heard, neither have entered into the heart of man, the things which God hath prepared for them that love him"* (1 Corinthians 2:9). Submitting to the direction of the Holy Spirit allows us to experience peace in our situations, *"the peace that transcends beyond all understanding"* according to Philippians 4:7. Developing the ability to look up from every problem, uncertainty, trial, adversity, worry, struggle, and all that is unavoidable, is essential to life because we have no life without Christ.

Following Christ does not mean that we will no longer share our feelings with a trusted friend or family member. God places certain people in our lives for encouragement and support just as we encourage and support others. Likewise, it does not mean that we will never shed a tear when life seems too heavy to bear? In this life, tears are a human reaction that allows us to release some of the weight of our situations, whereas looking to God gives us hope to overcome them. These human reactions are less frequent as our faith in God grows stronger.

In the midst of any situation, glorifying God transfers our thoughts and emotions from all that is happening and keeps us focused on Him, as He is in complete control. How do we move from a *spirit of distraction* to a *spirit of praise?* The technique of "Using the Upside of the Brain" steers us in the right direction. As we become confident in Christ we dismiss impatience, negativity, and any misunderstandings that emerge from our prideful expectations. We begin to allow the Truth (Jesus Christ) to open our eyes to a new perspective.

For instance, in life we may not always make the best choices. Sometimes the results of our choices reveal areas that we need to work on to avoid the situations they produce. As we choose to glorify God by building a relationship with Christ, we begin to live more effectively, even in the midst of our situations. Thus, living effectively is not whether God lifts us up out of our situations, but whether we lift God up [glorify Him] by our faith in Him. When we look to glorify God, we demonstrate our faith in Him because He is our only hope in every situation. Then our lives are more effective through Christ who gives us strength (Philippians 4:13).

The Apostle Paul clearly summarized the basis of "Using the Upside of the Brain" when he said,

> "*11According to the eternal purpose which he purposed [planned] in Christ Jesus our Lord: 12In whom we have boldness and access with confidence by the faith of him. 13Wherefore I desire that ye faint not at my tribulations for you, which is your glory. 14For this cause I bow my knees unto the Father of our Lord Jesus Christ, 15Of whom the whole family in heaven and earth is named, 16That he would grant you, according to the riches of his glory, to be strengthened with might by his Spirit in the inner man; 17That Christ may dwell in your hearts by faith; that ye, being rooted and grounded in love, 18May be able*

to comprehend with all saints what is the breadth, and length, and depth, and height; ¹⁹And to know the love of Christ, which passeth knowledge, that ye might be filled with all the fullness of God. ²⁰Now unto him that is able to do exceeding abundantly above all that we ask or think, according to the power that worketh in us, ²¹Unto him be glory in the church by Christ Jesus throughout all ages, world without end. Amen." (Ephesians 3:11-21).

Comments | "Using the Upside of the Brain"

Never a Dull Moment

I ONCE READ a comment posted by a frustrated individual on one of the popular social networks on the Internet. She asked, *"Why does life stink so much?"* Having several unfavorable experiences myself, I can certainly understand her frustration. Sometimes life seems to catch you off-guard. While putting out one fire, something else is about to ignite. What keeps me from getting discouraged is a growing relationship with Christ, because in Christ there is rest from our heavy burdens (Matthew 11:28-30).

Over the years I see that the more time I spend studying God's Word, praying, and most of all, learning to see my situations from God's perspective (Psalm 113:5,6), the more I understand that in life there is *never a dull moment.* Trials are expected (1 Peter 4:12,13). There will always be someone or something that needs attention, something that needs to be fixed or finished, or something that needs to be acquired for living. Those who *seem* to have everything going for them may only have what others desire. There are things that they are seeking too. Not everybody wants or needs the same things, but generally everybody wants what they don't already possess, though it is not always monetary or of quantitative value. It can be the desire to spend more time with family and friends or to have the benefit of good health. The philosophy of the world seems to cry out, *"it's never enough,"* possibly because we are focused on what is happening to us or not happening for us, rather than allowing our situations to draw us closer to God.

All that I can say is . . . "keep moving, keep praying, keep forgiving, keep hoping, keep standing, keep building, keep singing, keep laughing, keep loving, keep living, but most of all keep growing closer to the One who lifts us up when life knocks us down." Christ said *"These things I have spoken unto you, that in me ye might have peace. In the world ye shall have tribulation: but be of good cheer; I have overcome the world"* (John 16:33).

The trials we experience prove that God's Word is true because trials are a part of life. Furthermore, knowing that Christ is the Risen Savior, we must not live a defeated life or maintain a defeated outlook. Instead, rather than focus on our difficulties, we must focus on the difference we can make for Christ.

Comments | Never a Dull Moment

The Greatest Investment

When I think of investments, I think of stocks, bonds, CDs, and mutual funds. When I think of the definition of investment, I think of trading current assets for future benefits that an investor hopes to receive. Investing seems to require at least three actions: (1) belief that what you are investing in has greater value than what you already have, (2) willingness to sacrifice something you currently value for future benefits, and (3) commitment to the investment regardless of any change(s) in your ability to make the sacrifice or any conditions that appear to affect your investment. In other words, you are confident in your investment no matter what, because you have faith that your reward is greater than what you currently possess.

There are a couple of points I would like to make about investments. First, not every investment starts with a financial commitment. For instance, we also invest our time and talents when we work to earn a living or share our faith to bring others to Christ. Second, investments are not always about receiving *more* of something that we value. Sometimes we invest for the benefit of others. In any case, the benefits are only received if the investment is made.

Considering investments, only one is absolutely certain *and* everlasting. This investment is a relationship with Christ. Investing in possessions, family, friends, and even oneself is fine, but will not yield a comparable return. Therefore, *"Set your affection on things above, not on things on the earth"* (Colossians 3:2). In other words, *"19Lay not up for yourselves treasures upon earth, where moth and rust doth corrupt, and where thieves break through and steal: 20But lay up for yourselves treasures in heaven, where neither moth nor rust doth corrupt, and where thieves do not break through nor steal: 21For where your treasure is, there will your heart be also"* (Matthew 6:19-21).

We *cannot earn* eternal life with God (Ephesians 2:8-9) because it is freely given by the precious blood of Jesus Christ. We *can invest* in our relationship with Christ and reap the benefits of living more effectively by exercising our faith in Him. We can also invest in the lives of others by sharing the Word of God and demonstrating His love through our lives. *"3For this is good and acceptable in the sight of God our Saviour; 4Who will have all men to be saved, and to come unto the knowledge of the truth"* (1 Timothy 2:3,4). A relationship with Christ is the GREATEST INVESTMENT we could ever make because we are confident that our reward is greater than anything we could ever possess.

Comments | The Greatest Investment

I Believe That Was Yesterday

FORGIVENESS IS ONE of the most intriguing processes of life. For some individuals, it is not as difficult as it is for others who need time to figure it out. At some point, we all have to decide whether to forgive (Colossians 3:12,13) or hold on to feelings of resentment and anger towards others who have offended us. Sometimes we have to forgive ourselves for missed opportunities or other regrets.

When we struggle with forgiveness, we are deceived to think that we are in control of when the offender should be released from our judgment. We convince ourselves that if we forgive them, we agree or accept their offense and set them free to offend us again. Yet we are the ones held captive by holding on to the situation and allowing it to consume our thoughts, time, and energy.

Forgiveness is essential for spiritual well-being. It allows us to release negative emotions that keep us from functioning as productively as we were designed. Though we know we must forgive as our Father in Heaven forgives us (Matthew 6:14), it is sometimes difficult to let go because deep down inside, we are more concerned that the offender should pay for the wrong that was committed, and not be excused so easily. We feel this way because we have forgotten or do not really understand that the debt was already paid through the blood of Jesus Christ, Who died to take away our sins—*that which separates us from God* (Isaiah 59:2). His sacrifice demonstrated His love and forgiveness towards us, and through Christ we have life—a life we can freely receive that we do not deserve (Ephesians 2:8).

When we choose not to forgive, we hold on to what has happened in the past as if we have the power and authority to condemn. On the contrary, all power and authority belongs to the Lord (Matthew 28:18). Only He is able *to repay those who do evil against us* (Romans 12:19). For those whom He loves, He forgives because His love is unconditional (Romans 5:8; Romans 8:38,39). When we learn to love others unconditionally, we realize that whatever happened in the past stays in the past—never to resurface or linger.

Instead of struggling with forgiveness, pray and ask God to help you forgive. Take your focus off the offense or offender, and turn the matter over to God. Stop *"trying"* to forgive and instead, allow the Holy Spirit to repair your heart so you *"can"* forgive. The best way to truly forgive others is to love God more than ever for forgiving your sins. Remember, though we seek to follow the model life that Christ demonstrated, everyone falls short of God's glory (Romans 3:23).

Therefore, we must forgive as we are forgiven by the Lord. In doing so, we will no longer waste time and energy focusing on what was in the past. Instead, we will begin to realize that there are more yesterdays than there are tomorrows because tomorrow is not promised (Proverbs 27:1; Romans 13:10,11). If you struggle with forgiveness, let it go (Philippians 3:13,14). You are no longer bound to the past because *that was yesterday.*

Comments | I Believe That Was Yesterday

What Did You Learn?

Though my sisters and I live in different cities, we enrich each other's lives with our unique personalities and talents. One way or another, in our conversations, gestures, celebrations, and even disagreements, we all have something to contribute to each other's lives, if for no more than to remind each other how to love unconditionally.

I have some amazing sisters who are all gifts from God, and who have made my life more meaningful and complete. We may not always see eye to eye, but in every aspect I ultimately learn more of how God wants me to be—not only as a sister, but as a child of God (Galatians 3:26). I thank God for all of my sisters because we always learn something from each other, even in the most unexpected ways.

During a recent phone conversation with one of my sisters as I shared an adverse situation of my life, surprisingly, she responded by asking if I had learned anything from my experience. For a quick second, I tried to think if there was anything in particular that I had learned, and I immediately responded by saying, *"I'm stronger!"* After allowing me to give my most cliché response she agreed that spiritual strength in adversity is a great achievement. Still, she wanted to know if I learned anything in particular—something specific to draw from my situation that would make a difference in my life.

I thought a little further this time but could not pinpoint anything at the moment. So, I told her *"I'm pretty sure I learned something because I always believe that there is a reason for everything."* I just could not recall anything at the moment. After further consideration I responded by saying, *"Maybe I already used what I learned and now that it's over, I forgot."* To that response she replied *"Or maybe you haven't had the opportunity to use it yet."*

Finally, I started to realize that this conversation played a significant role in restructuring my entire view of adversity. Whether she intended to or not, with such a simple honest question she really gave me something to think about. I realized that adversity actually stimulates communication with God (Jonah 2:1,2). It gives you a reason to call on God, give Him your undivided attention, and then follow His lead to accomplish His purpose (Psalm 143:10).

Sometimes we get so caught up in trying to move beyond a situation that we overlook the positive nuances that it has to offer—the subtle lessons we can learn if we take the time to consider them.

Comments | What Did You Learn?

Live Like We Are Saved

WE ARE SAVED by the blood that Jesus Christ shed when He was crucified at a place called Golgotha (Matthew 27:33; Mark 15:22), also called Calvary (Luke 23:33). The purpose of this incredible sacrifice was to redeem humanity[3] through the forgiveness of our sins (Ephesians 1:7). As a result of this sacrifice, we are given the gift of a brand new life (2 Corinthians 5:17). This gift of salvation not only included the Gentiles during Biblical times, but also generations to come. However, since we have been given a choice, not everyone will accept salvation through Christ. Some will follow Him while others will follow the world. It is God's desire to have *"⁴. . . all men to be saved, and to come unto the knowledge of the truth. ⁵For there is one God, and one mediator between God and men, the man Christ Jesus;"* (1 Timothy 2:4,5).

How do we receive this priceless gift? If we confess that the Lord Jesus Christ is the Son of God and believe with all our heart that God raised Him from the dead we are saved (Romans 10:9,10; Acts 16:31). Only Christ could pay a debt that would pardon the sins of humanity[3] because He is sinless (2 Corinthians 5:21). In doing so, He saved us from the bondage of sin and the consequence of eternal death (Matthew 25:41,46; 2 Thessalonians 1:9), from which there is no hope of a future life with Christ.

By accepting the gift of salvation, we are admitting that we have been living a life in sin and now choose to turn our lives over to Jesus Christ as our Lord and Savior. The Lord said *"I, even I, am the Lord; and beside me there is no saviour"* (Isaiah 43:11). Christ is the only Way to our Heavenly Father (John 14:6), and by confessing our sins we are forgiven and cleansed for God's service (1 John 1:9). With Christ as our Savior we must also allow Him to be our Lord in order to live a productive life that is pleasing to God.

Furthermore, as Christians we must take care not to *claim* but rather *accept* Christ as our Lord and Savior. There is no commitment in merely claiming to know Christ and then continuing to live a self-willed life. Claiming Christ only means verbally asking Him to come into your life rather than allowing Him to take complete control. When we accept Christ as our Lord and Savior we are committed to the will of God and begin to establish a relationship with His Son, Jesus Christ, whereby we are accepted by Him (2 Corinthians 5:9). Then we begin to grow spiritually and take on His character as we learn to live our lives with confidence in Christ. *"[17]Herein is our love made perfect, that we may have boldness in the day of judgment: because as he is, so are we in this world. [20]If a man say, I love God, and hateth his brother, he is a liar: for he that loveth not his brother whom he hath seen, how can he love God whom he hath not seen?"* (1 John 4:17,20). By submitting to God's will, we allow Christ to reign as He is not only our Savior but also Lord over every aspect of our lives.

Establishing a relationship with Christ begins when we accept Him as our Savior. The relationship continues to grow when we accept Him as our Lord. As a result, not only can we live eternally with our Heavenly Father, but until then, we can live out the rest of our earthly lives saved and free from the bondage of sin. By accepting this precious gift of life, we are no longer slaves to sin, which results in death (Romans 6:23).

Even after receiving the gift of salvation, Christians sometimes forget what an awesome gift they have received. Though our sins have been forgiven, we still sometimes carry the *weight of sin*—a spiritual representation of the cross Christ already endured (Hebrews 12:1,2). Likewise, when we are reminded of our mistakes or poor choices we cover ourselves in guilt and shame, so much so, that we stop focusing on God. This guilt and shame becomes an even greater burden when we allow it to affect our relationships with others. We either withdraw or lash out in fear that others will judge or condemn us. Such a reaction suggests that we forgot our covering in that Christ died to reconcile us to God (Romans 5:6-10).

We must remember that we give sin power over us when we dwell on our issues or try to take matters into our own hands. The more time we spend dwelling on the past, the less we are thinking about the things of God that the Apostle Paul mentioned, "*Finally, brethren [believers in Christ], whatsoever things are true, whatsoever things are honest [honorable], whatsoever things are just, whatsoever things are pure, whatsoever things are lovely, whatsoever things are of good report; if there be any virtue, and if there be any praise, think on these things*" (Philippians 4:8).

Deuteronomy 7:11-14 expresses that God will bless, above all people, those who follow His commandments. We follow God's commandments not to avoid physical death as with those who lived during Old Testament times, but rather to avoid spiritual death (eternal separation from God), and to live more effectively while we are on Earth. God's commandments teach us His will for our lives and help keep us from yielding to temptations or struggles that we could otherwise avoid (Jonah Chapter 1).

We who have received the incredible gift of salvation must *live the love* that God has shown towards us (John 3:16) for we are recipients of the most priceless treasure ever to behold. Therefore, because we are saved, forgiven and redeemed by the blood of Jesus Christ, we must remember to live like we are saved.

Comments | Live Like We Are Saved

Point of Reference

ONE DAY I was driving along the highway relaxed, listening to music, and feeling very confident in the route I was taking until I took a wrong turn. It was definitely the wrong way because it started to look very unfamiliar.

Instead of turning around I thought maybe I would start recognizing the area soon. Yet, the further I drove the more I was lost, and the more I could not recover my point of reference. I didn't have a GPS (Global Positioning System for navigation). At that point, all I could do was pray that God would lead me to where I was supposed to be (Psalm 27:11).

Then I suddenly noticed how this whole ordeal resembled a life without Christ. Those who are unsaved[7] continue going their own way until they finally realize they are lost and need the Savior. When you are on the highway of life without Christ, you are without the guidance of the Holy Spirit who helps you relocate your point of reference. Your spiritual GPS (*God Perfecting System*) is the *application of God's Holy Word through the guidance of the Holy Spirit* (See page 25).

Even the saved[5] from time to time forget to refer to their spiritual GPS and end up taking a wrong turn occasionally. Like sheep, from time to time we all *go astray, trying to find our own way* (Isaiah 53:6). Those who accept Christ as their Lord and Savior are safely placed back on their path once they submit to the guidance of the Holy Spirit, while those who reject Christ continue to roam in darkness until they come to the saving knowledge of Jesus Christ. When the saved[5] veer off course, the Holy Spirit helps them locate *a new route* to regain their point of reference. This service is only available for those who establish an active relationship with Christ.

Going astray doesn't always refer to choices that are socially or morally inappropriate, but also any time we disregard God's plan for our own. It can be as personal as giving up on what God has called us to do, or as public as ignoring the opportunity to lead others to Christ. However, it is our choice to either follow the temptation and go the wrong way, or take heed to the warning signs and remain on course. The more we come to know Christ the more we recognize the warning signs of the Holy Spirit. Those who take a wrong turn recognize that they are not where they should be, and it is up to them to make the right choice and turn back.

Because of God's love, mercy, and grace, we are given another opportunity to get back on track when we go the wrong way. We can repent and turn away from anything that separates us from God (Mark 6:12; Hosea 14; Isaiah 55:6,7) by first *admitting our mistakes because the Lord is faithful and just to cleans us from all unrighteousness* (1 John 1:9). Turning away will not cost us our salvation because Christ paid the price once and for all (1 Peter 3:18), though this is not to say that we can keep turning away from God and going down the wrong path.

As recipients of God's grace we are saved (Ephesians 2:8,9) and forgiven. In 2 Chronicles 7:14 the Lord said, *"If my people, which are called by my name, shall humble themselves, and pray, and seek my face, and turn from their wicked ways, then will I hear from heaven, and will forgive their sin, and will heal their land."* Your land in this day and age could be your health, your career, your family, or even your finances.

Whether we take a wrong turn intentionally or unintentionally, we may have to face consequences of our actions even though we are forgiven so we may mature spiritually. Turning away places us in a very vulnerable or even dangerous position. The only way back is to regain our point of reference (Jesus Christ) through the Holy Spirit, and return to the Lord once and for all.

Comments | Point of Reference

God Perfecting System (GPS)

> *"[16]All scripture is given by inspiration of God, and is profitable for doctrine, for reproof, for correction, for instruction in righteousness: [17]That the man of God may be perfect [complete], throughly [completely] furnished unto all good works"* (2 Timothy 3:16,17).

A spiritual GPS (*God Perfecting System) is the study and application of God's Holy Word through the guidance of the Holy Spirit* for a more productive journey of life. Your reliable Service Provider is the Holy Spirit who activates God's Holy Word within you to help you stay on course.

How does it work? When you receive Christ as your Lord and Savior the Holy Spirit resides within you (1 Corinthians 3:16) to: guide you through the uncertainties of life (John 16:13); help you understand how to apply God's principles; and keep you moving forward according to the purpose God has planned specifically for you. Read and study the Word of God regularly to keep it current in your heart, spirit and mind for optimal navigation.

> *"And the spirit of the Lord shall rest upon him, the spirit of wisdom and understanding, the spirit of counsel and might, the spirit of knowledge and of the fear [reverence] of the Lord;"* (Isaiah 11:2).

GPS Service Specifications

Description: The Holy Spirit is a Person. Do not refer to the Holy Spirit as *"it."* The Bible refers to the Holy Spirit as *"He."*

"[16]And I will pray the Father, and he shall give you another Comforter, that he may abide [stay] with you for ever; [17]Even the Spirit of truth;

whom the world cannot receive, because it seeth him not, neither knoweth him: but ye know him; for he dwelleth with you, and shall be in you" (John 14:16,17).

He is a Sacred Being who comes into your heart when you receive Christ as your Lord and Savior. He will *teach* you how to follow Christ effectively.

"Thou gavest also thy good spirit to instruct them, . . ." (Nehemiah 9:20a)

"For the Holy Ghost shall teach you in the same hour what ye ought to say" (Luke 12:12)

Special Features. The Holy Spirit:

- Is One with God (Matthew 28:19)
- Was present with God in the beginning (Genesis 1:1-2,26)
- Has the attributes of God
  - ➢ Eternal (Hebrews 9:14)
  - ➢ Omnipresent (Psalms 139:7-10)
  - ➢ Omniscient (Isaiah 40:13; 1 Corinthians 2:10,11)
  - ➢ Omnipotent (Psalm 104:30; Romans 15:13)
- Yet, also has a distinct personality (Matthew 12:31, 32; John 14: 16; 16:5-15)

Accessories provided with this service. The Holy Spirit is equipped as:

- Truth (John 14:17; 15:26; 16:13)
- Grace (Zechariah 12:10; Hebrews 10:29)
- Holiness (Romans 1:4)
- The Comforter (John 14:26; 15:26)
- Producer of Good Fruit (Galatians 5:22,23)

Compliance. The Holy Spirit will be your guide as long as you listen and allow Him to lead (Romans 8:14). He will empower you to have victories (Romans 8:13; Galatians 5:16).

Remember to keep your GPS updated and always with you.

Walk It Out

GOD OUR HEAVENLY Father is truly the everlasting God, King above all, Lord forever. We can completely trust Him because He always stays true to His Word and never changes (James 1:17). We change. Sometimes we get tired of waiting for God and we start trying to work things out ourselves, only to end up getting in the way. It's true. We realize it when we see the struggles we cause for ourselves. Then we start wondering why God allows us to stumble from time to time.

I remember times in my life when I felt as if God left me to figure things out on my own, or He wasn't listening when I prayed. Nothing I would try was the answer, and it seemed as if God was watching me run aimlessly in circles. Then after I had exhausted all my options, I was finally ready to pay attention. That's when I realized that God actually has everything under control.

Before this realization, I would usually try to determine when and how I felt a situation should be resolved. Yet, all that I was actually doing was getting stressed over my plans instead of walking out God's plan in faith (Jeremiah 29:11). My plans were merely distractions that kept me occupied until I was ready to move forward with God leading the way. It took a while, but I finally learned that God really knows what He is doing. He doesn't need my input, advice, or permission.

God wants us to successfully complete the journey He set before us. That's why He so graciously provides everything that we need and even *some of the desires of our heart* (Psalm 37:4). If ever we feel discouraged and wonder why God seems so distant, all we have to do is trust Him enough to walk out the plan that He has for us with confidence in knowing that He is with us every step of the way.

Comments | Walk It Out

What Was That All About?

These days, all it takes is the loss of a job
amid an economic downturn *and the story begins.*

THERE ONCE WAS a man named Adam Webner. Now as you may guess, he really doesn't exist, at least not the Adam Webner to which I am referring. His character and his life were created to demonstrate faith and endurance, commitment and love—specifically to demonstrate a situation just right for "Using the Upside of the Brain," *to the extreme.*

Adam is a devout Christian man in his mid-thirties. He is married and together he and his wife have three children. He has a wonderful job and works diligently to take care of his family. Though he committed his life to Christ years ago at the age of 13, he continues to strengthen his relationship with Christ by reading the Bible daily during his lunch breaks. He praises God for *everything*—in the good times and the tough times. He prays about *everything* because Christ is his foundation.

He shares his faith with others, especially with those who come to him for encouragement because they see that his actions exemplify his faith in God. He leads his family to church for Sunday worship, midweek Bible study, and additional faith-based activities because he loves to worship God and study with other believers in Christ (Psalm 107:32). As a result, he and his wife and children have several opportunities for spiritual development.

His wife also loves God with all her heart. She faithfully serves God and supports her husband. Even their children demonstrate their love for God by loving and respecting their parents. For the most part, Adam lives what some people may refer to as a *storybook life,* or what I refer to as *a life after God's own heart.* Though everything appears to suggest a life of pure joy, as with everything on this Earth, this too shall pass (Deuteronomy 4:30, 31; 1 Peter 4:12-13; Romans 5:3; Ephesians 3:13, 14; 1 Peter 1:7; Acts 9:15, 16; 2 Corinthians 1:3-7; John 16:33).

One night as Adam and his wife were about to turn in for the evening she told him that the company where she was employed had started the first wave of layoffs. Of course, she was included in this group of unsuspecting individuals. She then continued to mention that she also learned that she was expecting their fourth child. They both were very excited to know that they would soon have another child, but they were concerned about how the layoff would affect their finances. However, as always, Adam assured his wife that everything will be just fine.

A little preoccupied the next morning, Adam drove too fast on the way to work and was directed by a police officer to pull over to the side of the road for speeding. When the police officer approached the car he noticed that the inspection sticker on Adam's car had expired, which also contributed to the violation. Adam waited patiently for the police officer to finish writing the ticket and then Adam proceeded to work more attentive.

Shortly after he arrived he was called into his supervisor's office. Contrary to what seems most likely to happen next, he was not laid off. Instead, he was asked to lay off twelve other employees. When Adam returned home from work that evening he was grateful to keep his job, but discouraged with the thought of his fellow employees losing their jobs by the end of the week. Moreover, he was troubled about having to be the one to let them go especially after his wife recently lost her job.

Adam prayed that God would give him strength and help him stay focused. He trusted God to see him through because he knew that God was in complete control. He also prayed for his family and for the families of his fellow employees who would be affected by the company's drastic decision.

By the end of the week Adam had spoken with every employee he was asked to lay off. Then, at about 5:10 p.m., Adam starting getting ready to go home. He walked past his supervisor's office who called out to him to hold the elevator. They rode down several floors together in total silence. The moment seemed to last forever. When Adam's supervisor stepped off the elevator, he turned and handed Adam an envelope and said *"Have a good evening Adam."* Walking to his car, Adam started to put the envelope in his pocket but decided to wait. Curious about what just happened, he got into his car, buckled his seatbelt, and began to read the letter. *"Wow!"* he thought. Obviously he was laid off too!

After dinner when their children went outside to play, Adam told his wife about the letter. Puzzled, yet not surprised, they both sat at the dining room table trying to process their thoughts of all that had happened.

A few weeks later his wife learned that she wasn't expecting after all. Instead, she was diagnosed with having GTD (Gestational Trophoblastic Disease), a rare tumor that can simulate pregnancy. Though generally curable, it can be fatal. Because they were both unemployed there was no medical insurance and disability through Social Security could take up to three months to process. At this point, all they could do was to continue praying as they looked to God for strength and her healing.

After several months, money was extremely tight even with both their unemployment benefits. They barely had enough to meet the expenses they regularly incur. Then when Adam was able to find contract work, the income, of course, was deducted from his benefits. By now their savings account was nearly drained and with both unemployed they had no medical insurance to cover the expenses his wife was accumulating.

With such a downturn in the economy Adam was overqualified for the jobs that were available, leaving their house at risk for foreclosure. Because they were unable to make the payments, their cars were repossessed. Using the last of their savings Adam bought a used car and in a few weeks it started having major problems. Then, when the inspection sticker expired he could barely afford to get the car repaired to pass the requirements.

By now his wife had become fatally ill and there was nothing much that they could do to change their situation. In spite of all the setbacks and disappointments, Adam continued to pray and remain focused on God through these tests of faith (Proverbs 17:3). He knew that however God decided to let these events unfold, he loved God even more because he believed that everything God had given him belonged to God—his life, his family, and his possessions. After several attempts to control the disease his wife succumbed to the inevitable. As Adam fixed his focus on God, trusting that He knew what was best, he was totally at peace (Romans 5:1).

Many people would wonder why God didn't heal Adam's wife or at least improve their situation. This faithful believer trusted and depended on God and yet the outcome looks like God let him down. When we hear stories or situations such as this, we feel frustrated, disappointed, and somewhat forsaken because we still see our lives as our own possession. Just as we cannot tell others how to manage their plans; we cannot tell God how to manage His plans. Isaiah 55:8-9, clearly states, *"⁸For my thoughts are not your thoughts, neither are your ways my ways, saith the Lord. ⁹For as the heavens are higher than the earth, so are my ways higher than your ways, and my thoughts than your thoughts."*

So, *"What was that all about?"* We may never know. Because we can only see what appears to be happening, we don't always understand the situation from our perspective. *"For who hath known the mind of the Lord? or who hath been his counselor?"* (Romans 11:34). God is our Creator and He knows exactly what He is doing. He doesn't need our input or our approval *"For of him, and through him, and to him, are all things: to whom be glory for ever. Amen"* (Romans 11:36).

When we look for God to work things out by our expectations we miss the whole purpose of His plan. Think of it this way. The religious leaders during Biblical times prided themselves in believing that they knew the Messiah based on their interpretation of the prophecies of His coming. Yet because they relied on their expectations, they chose not to believe and accept Jesus of Nazareth as the Christ, the Son of the Living God. Since that day, people have rejected Jesus Christ because they refuse to acknowledge Him as their Lord and Savior. They hide behind the misconception that if God is who Christians claim Him to be, then how can He allow so much suffering in this world?

Similar to these same religious leaders, people today who struggle with God's sovereignty tend to measure what happens in life from their perspective. They look for God to please them instead of seeking to please God. That is why anything that happens contrary to their expectations leads them to doubt or reject Christ.

Considering many escalating worldwide disasters, the unsaved[7] and even sometimes the saved[5] immediately blame God and criticize Him as though He fails to protect and care for the lives He created. From all that we learn by reading the Bible and through personal life experiences, we as Christians know that God has never and will never fail. God doesn't chastise us out of hatred, spite, or without cause. The Bible tells us that *"The just Lord is in the midst thereof; he will not do iniquity: every morning doth he bring his judgment to light, he faileth not; but the unjust knoweth no shame"* (Zephaniah 3:5). No matter how spiritually depraved the world may be, *"God is our refuge and strength, a very present help in times of trouble"* (Psalm 46:1).

Despite what some people choose to believe, God doesn't want us to suffer. The pains that we endure are generally products of a sinful world (i.e., war, poverty, and disease). God only allows us to endure what will make us stronger and what will bring about the end results that are necessary to fulfill His Master Plan. Thus, as a loving parent, God endures the pain of seeing His children learn life lessons through trial and error.

Even though we may not understand or even agree with God's plan, know that in every situation we have an opportunity to demonstrate complete faith in God no matter what. If we keep our eyes focused on Him, we won't ever wonder about His plan. We will praise Him because He is the Almighty God. He said, *"Be still, and know that I am God:...I will be exalted in the earth"* (Psalm 46:10).

Comments | What Was That All About?

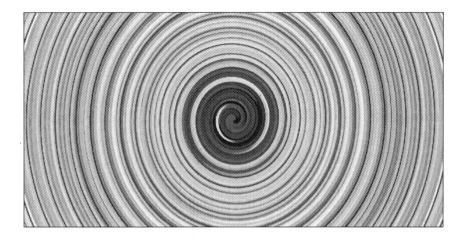

Spiritual Ailments Part 1: Defined

Obedience to God's Word sustains our physical health (Proverbs 4:20-22) by allowing us to lead a healthy spiritual life in Christ. Thus, we are more productive in carrying out God's plan so that our lives may encourage others to come to Christ. *"³For this is good and acceptable in the sight of God our Saviour; ⁴Who will have all men[3] to be saved[5], and to come unto the knowledge of the truth* (1 Timothy 2:3,4). God's plan is outlined in the Holy Bible, of which there are several translations available for understanding the Scriptures. As we study God's Word we learn the difference between what is of God and what is of humanity³. Then we are able to recognize temptations that lead to sin (Isaiah 59:2). If we choose not to take heed, we leave ourselves open to spiritual ailments.

As there are physical ailments that attack our physical body, there are spiritual ailments that attack our spiritual life. Everyone is susceptible to a spiritual ailment by virtue of the human tendency to sin (Isaiah 64:6).

What is a spiritual ailment? Associating it with the definition of a physical ailment, I came to the conclusion that a spiritual ailment is *the condition of yielding to anything that disrupts our relationship with*

Christ and hinders spiritual growth. Three of the more common spiritual ailments that attack and weaken spiritual health are complacency, doubt, and conceited pride. They function as a malignant and invasive growth with symptoms such as self-will, deception, and greed, causing us to resist the will of God and become spiritually unproductive. If left untreated: for those who are saved[5], it can delay the blessings that sustain health, family, business, and possessions; and for those who are unsaved[7], it can become spiritually fatal.

Biblically speaking, complacency is the state of showing no need for God or the desire to build a relationship with Christ. Unintentionally, complacent Christians may demonstrate an attitude of unconcern or self-sufficiency. They convince themselves that there is no need to worry God about a particular situation or to move forward on what God is leading them to do. For instance, though God may be giving them countless opportunities to minister to others, they choose to wait until they feel that they are ready. As for the unsaved[7], though they are recently introduced to the love of Christ through hearing God's Word, they choose to continue living their own lives while they think they still have time. In either case with the saved[5] or unsaved[7], there is a lack of commitment to or lack of interest in God respectively, coupled with self-satisfaction. God doesn't want us to worry or make hasty decisions, but He expects us to respond when He calls.

Like complacency, doubt also attacks our spiritual health. Doubt surfaces when we are not investing in our relationship with Jesus Christ. We know that God sent Jesus to be our Lord and Savior. Yet, because of several unfavorable experiences in our past, we sometimes wonder what God is doing or why He doesn't seem to be doing anything about our situation at hand. We must understand that even in such a turbulent world we can have peace and never doubt God's presence or His response. Jesus said in John 16:33, *"These things I have spoken unto you, that in me ye might have peace. In the world ye shall have tribulation: but be of good cheer; I have overcome the world."* This means that God is in complete control, and we can trust His promises (Numbers 23:19; Romans 3:4; Proverbs

3:5,6). Furthermore, whatever we go through is not necessarily because of anything that we have done against God. Sometimes situations occur simply because we live in a sinful world. Even still, the power of God will be made known (John 9:1-7) because of the victory we have through Christ.

Though we may face the consequences of our actions, Christ already paid the debt of sin when He died on the cross, was buried, and rose from the dead. Therefore, we belong to God and He promised to see us through every situation we face. By this we have confidence in knowing that no matter how big or small the situation may appear, God cares (Psalm 55:22, and 1 Peter 5:7). Any doubt that we may have signifies that we need to invest more time in our relationship with Christ.

The third most common spiritual ailment comes in the form of *conceited pride*. A person stricken with conceited pride demonstrates excessive faith in himself or herself rather than in God. Pride, that graciously *edifies*[2] others, is acceptable—for instance, when you praise your child for doing well in school. Likewise, pride that humbly appreciates the results of your efforts is acceptable, as long as you give all glory to God, in that by Him you were able to prevail. However, conceited pride is self-destructive (1 Timothy 3:6; Proverbs 16:18,19;) and was the cause of Satan's downfall (Isaiah 14:12-20; Luke 10:18-19; 2 Peter 1:19).

Conceited pride is not ashamed because it doesn't recognize the act of being prideful. It doesn't care whether you live by affluent or humble means. It thrives on your desire to make others believe that you are at the level they should be: whether in finances, academics, or spirituality. Yes, even Christians can be infected by conceited pride. It starts with an honest desire to share the Word of God, and then turns into arrogant judgment and condemnation of others.

Spiritual ailments become more widespread if left untreated. They are always ready to strike. They are not like a physical ailment that God may choose to heal once and for all. They flare up in different forms whenever we let our guard down and become susceptible to sin. When we don't get enough rest, or feed our minds regularly with the Word of God, spiritual ailments attack. If you are experiencing a spiritual ailment, refocus on God and start your healing today. Jesus said, *". . . My grace is sufficient for thee: for my strength is made perfect in weakness"* (2 Corinthians 12:9).

Comments | Spiritual Ailments Part 1: Defined

Spiritual Ailments Part 2: Healing

As God's creation, we cannot endure life without Him. By not seeking God first (Matthew 6:33), we choose to follow our own way (Isaiah 53:6), which will eventually cause us to suffer spiritual ailments. When we acquire the symptoms, our minds and bodies will literally ache with the burden of stress, guilt, sorrow, and all sorts of emotions that surface while we are weak.

How does God heal us from spiritual ailments? First of all, remember that we are vulnerable when we take our eyes off Christ, even for just a second. That's why God wants us to keep our eyes fixed and focused on Him (Hebrews 12:2) and pray continually (1 Thessalonians 5:17).

We overcome spiritual ailments by committing our lives completely to God and investing in a faithful relationship with His Son, Jesus Christ. The more time we spend with the Lord, the stronger resistance we build to maintain our spiritual health. When Jesus said *"abide in me and I in you"* (John 15:4), He promised to stay with us even when we fail to stay with Him. When He seems far away, we feel isolated because we have actually left His presence. Yet, as long as we stay close and follow His lead we will be strong enough to fight off the symptoms, make better decisions, and be more productive. Though we may not always accomplish our goals immediately, we must be consistent in our walk with Christ because God expects us to make an honest effort to carry out His plan (1 Corinthians 4:2; Matthew 25:21).

Studying God's Word is a spiritually satisfying way to spend quality time with the Lord. It is how we mature in our walk with Christ and continue to grow closer to Him. God's Word sets us apart and prepares us for His service. Jesus said, *"Sanctify[A] them through thy truth: thy word is truth"* (John 17:17). The Truth is God's healing power that nourishes a hungry soul and helps maintain our spiritual health.

During a mid-week Bible study, Reverend Michael E. Woods of Wichita, Kansas shared an inspiring lesson that presented an effective analogy for maintaining spiritual health. He said, *"Diet is a major determining factor of the quality of one's physical health and well-being. Likewise, spiritual health and well-being can be greatly enhanced by the study, interpretation and practical application of God's word."* As we maintain the proper spiritual diet of Bible study, pray for understanding, and apply God's Word to our lives, we find the strength to resist spiritual ailments.

Prayer is essential (Hebrews 11:6) to maintain a faithful relationship with Christ. It personalizes our communication with God by allowing us to participate in the most significant relationship of our lives. Since God is our Heavenly Father (2 Corinthians 6:17,18), we should never approach Him mechanically out of routine. *"Blessed are the pure in heart: for they shall see God"* (Matthew 5:8). We sometimes associate prayer as a time we spend with the Lord before we go to sleep at night. Generally, we kneel down, fold our hands, bow our head, and close our eyes to acknowledge, worship, praise, and thank God, as well as make our petition. However, we can meet God anywhere, anytime, and about anything—whether we kneel, sit, or stand.

When we come into the presence of the Lord to pray, an effective approach is to: (1) **a**cknowledge and praise God for His Majestic Holiness, (2) **c**onfess our sins and ask for His forgiveness, (3) always remember to thank Him for all He has done and will do, and then (4) make our requests (supplications). This approach is a well-known acronym that spells the word A.C.T.S. When we pray we take action by coming to the Lord with our petitions and we seek action from the Lord through His response. Moreover, making requests in our prayers is not solely for our own needs, but also to intercede for the needs of others (Job 16:21; Genesis 18:16-33).

Although we commit our lives to the Lord and dwell in His presence through Bible study and prayer, we still face the uncertainties of life. Even so, we must stay focused in order to maintain a faithful relationship with Christ. Thus, for optimal spiritual healing, pray about everything, everywhere, all the time. This doesn't mean recite a bunch of elaborate religious sounding words while neglecting our job, family, and other responsibilities. Instead, stay in tune with God's Word, in your mind and your spirit throughout the day; remembering how God wants you to approach each situation by applying His Word. God loves to hear our voice when we pray, especially when we praise Him (Hebrews 13:15). But when our surroundings are not conducive to verbally speak the words of our prayer, we can always talk with God spiritually in our thoughts because God knows our thoughts and He knows us completely (Psalm 139:1,2).

As we build a faithful relationship with Christ we become more resistant to spiritual ailments. We find the courage to get out of our *boat* and do some amazing things to glorify God; just as Peter, a disciple of Jesus, was able to walk on water as long as he kept His eyes on Christ (Matthew 14:27-31). We begin to sink when we listen to the tempting voice of reason rather than the voice of Truth.

While building a relationship with Christ, certain challenging situations sometimes tempt us to respond in ways that are not spiritually productive. For instance, directing anger towards others or making wrong choices in life. If we think back through some of our experiences, we may recall a small voice from within that suggested an alternate response.

The voice of the Holy Spirit gives us discernment[1] to avoid making poor choices that we later regret.

During spiritual battles God knows what can attack us. Accordingly, through Christ we can overcome any situation and escape the burden of sin. In 1 Corinthians 10:13, the Apostle Paul wrote of how there is *no temptation that we could ever face, that God hasn't already made a way for us to overcome.* The only remedy for spiritual ailments is Jesus Christ. Those who are saved[5] can avoid flare ups by building a stronger relationship with Christ through studying God's Word and praying consistently. Those who are unsaved[7] can recover only by accepting Jesus Christ as their Lord and Savior and as a result avoid a spiritual fatality (Romans 6:23).

Comments | Spiritual Ailments Part 2: Healing

FALL SECTION

What's My Motivation?

"*. . . SEEK YE first the kingdom of God, and his righteousness; and all these things shall be added unto you"* (Matthew 6:33). What is your primary focus? Do you seek to *get the best* out of life rather than allow God to *bring out the best* in you? Is God merely the source of what you seek to acquire, or do you see Him as the source of your existence?

My primary focus is God. He wakes me up every morning and keeps me throughout the day. He is the only reason I live because He lives in me through Christ Jesus, my Lord and Savior (Galatians 2:20).

God is the Creator of all that is and ever will be. He is the Artist of a living Masterpiece titled "Life." I marvel at how He is so into detail. Nothing was created by accident or second thought. Every element was purposefully planned and carefully created. Though God is not a physical being (John 4:24), every now and then I get a glimpse of His presence in the way He takes care of everything that was once a concern.

No one has seen God (John 1:18), but He is always visibly present in the beauty of His creation that surrounds us—in a ray of sunshine that peaks beneath a gray cluster of clouds, or the wind that gently ruffles the leaves of a tree. He makes me smile whenever I look beyond the obvious and see His face in all that He has done. He doesn't have to solve every issue in my life all at once, though He has the power to do so if He chooses. I know from experience that He has everything under control.

God is the center of my life because God is love (1 John 4:8b). I truly love and praise God for His compassion, mercy, grace, and all His wonderful works (Psalm 107:8, 15, 21, and 31). His blessings come in many forms, not only what we anxiously request, but what He has generously provided that we sometimes take for granted. For instance, we are blessed with the use of our eyes, hands, legs, and feet. We are also blessed with the air that we breathe and the food that He provides daily (Matthew 6:11).

Because of God's unconditional love, these blessings are available even to those who have not come into the Light of salvation. Why? Because God created every one of us with our own unique purpose, and it is His compassionate desire that all will be saved (Matthew 18:11-14; 1 Timothy 2:1-4) to live eternally with Him.

Yet, even as believers, we sometimes take God for granted. We tend to appreciate Him most upon receipt of His blessings and neglect Him once the blessings are consumed or no longer of interest or urgency. If we fully understood who God is, we would never treat Him this way. Instead, we would continually praise God for being Who He Is (Exodus 3:14; Matthew 22:32; 1 John 4:8; John 4:24; Colossians 1:15-17; Psalm 47; Psalm 146:5-10; Exodus 32:9-14; Isaiah 9:6; John 14:6-10; John 5:22-23) and know that He is *a rewarder of those who diligently seek him* (Hebrews 11:6b). We can show our gratitude to God by seeking His face (2 Chronicles 7:14) and not His hand.

Sometimes we overlook God's blessings when we become more concerned with what other people possess or what we seem to be lacking. In such case, we are motivated by the gifts rather than the Giver.

Essentially, what motivates us exposes who we really are or where we are in our relationship with Christ. As we mature in Christ, the things of this world are no longer our *main* focus. This is not to say that we should never look to have some of the things that are of interest, but that

God will always provide everything that we need (Philippians 4:19). He already demonstrated the extent of His desire to bless us (Romans 8:32). Still, His blessings should not be our main focus. We must continually show gratitude to God with an appreciative heart giving thanks for all He has done (1 Thessalonians 5:18) because He has a specific purpose and plan for our lives.

Some people are not interested in God's plan because they think it will make their lives boring. Unlike what the unsaved[7] may believe, I can honestly say that God's plan doesn't keep me from enjoying life. It actually provides a whole new life I never knew I could enjoy. His plan is less complicated and causes less stress. As I continue to grow spiritually I realize that some of the things I thought I wanted in life I have outgrown.

Spiritual growth takes time. It develops as we experience life's challenges and learn to apply God's Word. Most of all it takes willingness to follow Christ even when it is inconvenient or not the popular choice.

What's my motivation? Praising God because He is worthy.

Comments | What's My Motivation?

Forever In My Heart

I REALLY MISS my mom. She passed away several years ago yet it seems like she is still alive in my hometown tending to the things that made her day complete. Though she is no longer in my presence I have peace knowing that she is in the presence of the Lord (2 Corinthians 5:8). She left this life with a body failing in health, and is now wearing a new body with a heavenly design (1 Corinthians 15:49-52). Because I know that she is no longer in pain and instead free from the cares of life on Earth, I have joy in spite of my loss. Though I miss being able to see her, she will be in my heart forever.

Losing a loved one can be as painful as losing a part of your own body—a part that you suddenly have to live without. Though we are temporarily apart (2 Corinthians 5:10), I may sometimes cry only because I miss having her here with me. It doesn't seem fair but it's a part of life that's inevitable.

At times physical death seems so final, as though there is nothing else after life as we know. Yet the more I grow spiritually, the more I understand that our physical death is essentially another blessing from God. When we leave this Earth, we can spend our eternal life at home safe and sound with the Lord. I can imagine it would be like coming home to the scent of fresh baked bread (John 6:58) after a long, exhausting journey. Life is not over when we surrender our mortal body in exchange for a glorified body like Christ received when He was resurrected (Philippians 3:20, 21). For those who accept Christ as their Lord and Savior, He is the doorway into the presence of God (John 10:7-9). It is comforting to know that when we leave this world we will live eternally with the Lord. Therefore, we love God even more because He faithfully keeps His promise of everlasting life (John 11:25,26; John 3:16; Hebrews 5:9).

There is so much more to life with God (Luke 23:43) than life as we know on Earth (Matthew 6:19). Knowing that one day we will be with the Lord is not about leaving loved ones behind, but rather finally receiving our heavenly reward (1 Corinthians 3:8; Revelations 22:12) for faithfully completing the tasks we have been given by God (John 17:4; Matthew 25:21) while on Earth. Yet, no matter how wonderful it sounds to be at home with the Lord, we can only complete our tasks on God's terms and in God's time.

Learning to deal with the loss of a loved one is not easy but possible if you understand that the people in your life are not created for you. We all belong to God (John 17:9,10) even though He graciously allows us the choice to accept His Son Jesus Christ as our Lord and Savior while we are here on Earth (Joshua 24:15). As we interact with our family and friends, they may make an impact in our lives one way or another, but we all have a specific purpose to fulfill over a specified period of time, and only God knows for how long. When we don't understand that we are all here on Earth for God's purpose and not our own, we may feel like God is taking a significant part of our lives away at the loss of our loved ones. Still, how can we say that God has taken them away from *"us"* when we all belong to God? He just let us borrow them for a little while to be a blessing to each other.

Ultimately, we must return what we've borrowed to fully enjoy what we have received. In as much as we are a blessing towards our loved ones, we are blessed by the memories of their lives forever.

Comments | Forever In My Heart

Reinforcing the Seems

> Don't stress over *the seems.*
> Without *thread,* they tend to fall apart.

THERE WERE TIMES in my life that seemed as though the more I looked to God the more I experienced greater trials and disappointments. I wondered why God seemed to send me through more hardships and uncertainties than what I thought anyone could bear. I knew that everyone, from time to time, will face moments in life that seem unbearable, but it just seemed to me that I had more than my share.

Seems Unbearable. I can recall a well-known saying suggesting that *God will not allow more than we can bear.* What is key in this statement is the word "*we.*" On our own we can do nothing, but through Christ we can do all things (Philippians 4:13). Because we belong to God, I believe that sometimes He purposefully allows more than we could bear *"on our own"* because He is always with us to see us through. Besides, the extra weight works our *muscle of faith* to further our spiritual growth. Essentially, we are exercising our faith in His Son Jesus Christ. The more we workout with Christ (Philippians 2:12-13), the more we are able to withstand the trials of life and be more effective witnesses for Him.

Moreover, I believe that this saying not only refers to our ability to handle the pressures of life, but also whether or not we are ready to handle *more blessings*. When we pray to God, we may not understand why God doesn't answer either in our timeframe or in the way that we expect. His silence may seem as though He doesn't care or He isn't listening even though we see our issue as urgent. Regardless, we must remember that God knows us better than we know ourselves (Psalm 139). When we use our blessings selfishly or neglect to use them at all (Matthew 25:14-30), we demonstrate that we are not ready to receive what we request. God doesn't want us to waste His blessings just as He doesn't want us to fail our tests (Philippians 1:6; James 1:12).

When God seems to be distant and not respond to your call, don't think that you are forsaken. This is your opportunity to exercise your faith. God wants you to trust that His blessings will come at the right time and for His glory.

Seems Forsaken. Additionally, there were times in my life that *seemed* as though the more I praise God and tell others about what He has done for me, the more difficult my life seemed to become. This was very awkward because I thought, "How can I tell the unsaved[7] that God will never forsake them when in my situations I seemed to be forsaken?" I must admit that I felt this way even though I knew the Lord promised to never leave me. He said in John 14:18, *"I will not leave you comfortless: I will come to you."*

Speaking out for Christ allows you to see just how much faith you have in Him. As you learn to depend on the Lord completely to help you plant the seed of faith in the lives of others, in the same process you also learn that God is growing the seed of faith someone planted in you.

God is not pleased when we keep looking back. He doesn't want us to keep turning away with every uncertainty. Like a child, in our spiritual immaturity we are as *"a double-minded man, unstable in all his ways"* (James 1:8). If to the unsaved[7] we appear to be forsaken by God, it is not because we are forsaken. It is because we failed to demonstrate faith that God will never forsake us.

Seems Unfair. When I first learned of God's sovereignty—that He has dominion, power, and authority over all—I struggled more with why God wouldn't fix my situations than I struggled with the situations themselves. During this early stage of my spiritual growth, God *seemed* to dangle hope right before my eyes at my greatest times of need. He seemed to withhold His blessings or keep me in an unfavorable situation longer than I felt was necessary. I also wondered why God seemed to allow tough times to last longer, or happen more often than the good times. I could hardly enjoy the more favorable moments because I knew the tough times would soon return. Then, as I continued studying and applying God's Word to my life I came to know Him on a more personal level. I began to learn how God loved me so much that He took the time to teach me about Himself and about life in general through the challenges I faced.

God is in control and we must submit to His will because He is God. To think that He *zaps* us with hardships every time we get out of line is to think that we have control over Him by getting out of line. God chastises our disobedience with love and mercy to lift us up, not whips and chains to bring us down. Thus, the trials we face are necessary so that our joy in the Lord will be complete (John 15:1-11).

Thread of Faith. As I continue to grow in my relationship with Christ, I learn to trust God more each day by applying God's Biblical principles to my personal situations. I draw strength from my life-changing experiences and begin to notice and appreciate how God is spiritually developing me more each day. I no longer focus on what *seems*. I focus on Christ who is the Son of the only TRUE and LIVING GOD (Psalm 18:46), ALMIGHTY KING, RULER OF HEAVEN AND EARTH, COMPASSIONATE, MERCIFUL, LOVER OF MY SOUL. No one can fully comprehend God's compassionate love. If they could then sin would not exist in the world today. God's love is unlike the love humans express—in most cases based on conditions. He shows His love time after time, because His love never fails (1 Corinthians 13:8; Psalm 136) and because He is Love (1 John 4:8 and 16).

We serve the GREATEST GOD, the MIGHTIEST GOD. *"Bless the Lord, O my soul. O Lord my God, thou art very great; thou art clothed with honour and majesty"* (Psalm 104:1). Though LARGER than we could ever imagine, God even takes the time to show us just how much He loves us when we ask anything of Him. He allows us to have a personal relationship with Him (Exodus 33:11-23) through Christ Jesus who demonstrated the greatest love ever by paying the price on the cross for our sins (John 3:16). His grace is sufficient (2 Corinthians 12:9) and His mercy endures forever (Psalm 136:2).

Therefore, when life seems to unravel, don't become frustrated and wonder if God really cares. Faith is the thread that reinforces *the seems.* It is *the substance of things hoped for and the evidence of things not seen* (Hebrews 11:1). Faith keeps you focused on what's really at hand so you can *"Trust in the Lord with all thine [your] heart; and lean not unto thine own understanding"* (Proverbs 3:5). Leaning on the *"seems"* only weakens your thread of faith. The stronger your thread of faith, the stronger bond you will have with Christ.

Comments | Reinforcing the Seems

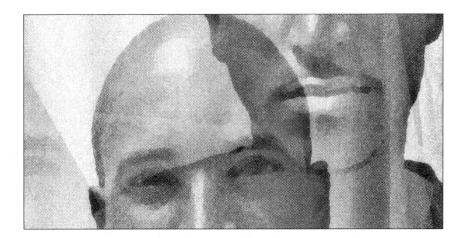

Think On These Things

Occasionally there are some things that may drop into your mind unannounced—*the Should Have, Could Have, and Would Have.* As precious as time can be, you can't spend too much time worrying about the past (Isaiah 43:18). When it comes to mind, depending on how you feel at the moment or how much of an impact it may have, it's your choice to dwell on that thought or move on.

At times, your thoughts may remind you of missed opportunities, unsuccessful efforts, or regrets. Unfortunately, no matter how great the issue, human nature tends to be more influenced by unfavorable moments because these moments tend to leave a more lasting impression. For instance, a tiny paper cut or a snide remark can have a greater impact on a person's day than a kind gesture or compliment. Why? I really don't know. Maybe it's the natural desire to succeed, and anything that gets in the way no matter how small, suddenly requires your full attention.

If the memory of a negative instance enters your mind, dismiss it by "Using the Upside of the Brain." Look up from the situation to clear your mind and focus on knowing that everything happens for a reason. Don't waste any more time thinking about something that already served its purpose or something you can't do anything about at this point. When you let go and release negative reminders, you will have room to effectively process more productive thoughts.

Next time a *Should Have, Could Have, and Would Have* tries to enter your mind, remember the *Been There* and *Done That* so you can move forward. Let your mind focus on the moments that make you smile. Let those moments go deep into your spirit and warm the cold crevices of past heartaches or misfortunes. Keep your mind focused on thoughts of progress and encouragement.

> *"⁸Finally, brethren, whatsoever things are true, whatsoever things are honest, whatsoever things are just, whatsoever things are pure, whatsoever things are lovely, whatsoever things are of good report; if there be any virtue, and if there be any praise, think on these things. ⁹Those things, which ye have both learned, and received, and heard, and seen in me, do: and the God of peace shall be with you"* (Philippians 4:8-9).

Comments | Think On These Things

Share Your Faith

MOST PEOPLE HAVE no problem sharing exciting news. They can hardly wait to share their joy about a new car, house, job, or new born baby. As Christians grow spiritually, we must remember that our primary responsibility is to spread the Gospel, the Good News of Jesus Christ (Matthew 28:19-20; Luke 24:47; Philippians 1:27; 2 Timothy 2:1-2). It is the most important news we could ever share.

Our life-changing experiences demonstrate the hope and strength that others may seek and that we sometimes take for granted. These experiences provide opportunities for us to be a witness chosen by God to let others know of His power and grace (Isaiah 43:9-11). Through Christ, we are the light for those who are in darkness (Romans 2:19). Yet instead of reaching out, many of us keep the Good News to ourselves. When we do not acknowledge the Lord's blessings, we essentially take credit for what He has done in our lives and risk losing the opportunity for another soul to be saved.

Why are we so passive in sharing our faith? We sometimes hesitate so not to offend others by making them uncomfortable with the truth of

God's Word. Maybe we want to avoid the rejection of those who refuse to hear what God has to say through us. Perhaps we fear being confronted with questions that we are unprepared to answer because we have not taken time to study God's Word. As we study regularly, we are more equipped to represent Christ effectively in an ever-changing world.

With all the distractions of the world, some Christians lose their passion for God's Word, and as a result, they lose their confidence to represent Christ. As long as sin is in the world, we must accept the call to tell others about our Lord. The more we share our faith the stronger our faith becomes.

There is a need for Christians to be strong and confident in Christ, willing to share how the Lord has made a difference in their lives and ready to help make a difference in the lives of others. Because the world seems to take a nonchalant attitude towards sin, the need for sharing the Gospel is greater than ever before. Those who have become accustomed to the world's standards tend to categorize sin by degrees or levels of guilt and shame. They condone the behavior of what they perceive as the "smaller" offenses in order to justify their personal desires and opinions. This mindset comes from focusing on what is most convenient for them, what they believe does not apply, what they fear others may say, or what they eventually learn to accept. Sin has no categories. All sin is displeasing to God. Like a small crack in a windshield, a slight increase in gasoline or food prices, or even a tiny paper cut, what may seem insignificant generally has a greater impact than what is expected. Whether major or minor to us, whatever God calls sin is sin. It is basically what He despises, what is against His name, or what He did not intend. Sin not only offends God, but negatively affects others.

As long as there is sin in the world, there are people who need to be saved. It is our responsibility as Christians to be the light that shines for Christ and share our faith so that others will come to know and love Jesus as their Lord and Savior. Once we make the effort, no matter how we feel about our abilities or the amount of spiritual knowledge we possess, we must share our faith.

Jesus said in Matthew 10:19, 20 that there is no need to worry about what to say or how to say it, because the Holy Spirit will guide us as we speak.

Sharing our faith makes us available to God as *His instruments of righteousness* (Romans 6:12,13) to help restore those who are lost, and to keep ourselves connected with Christ. We are the salt of the Earth (Matthew 5:13), the seasoning that brings out the flavor of God's Word in a bland and weary world. When we share our faith, the Lord replenishes hope and joy in those who are willing to receive Him. Their lives are transformed and they begin to experience the benefits of following Christ and living a life that is pleasing to God.

Having the responsibility to share our faith does not place us on a pedestal of perfection (Romans 3:23) or give us the right to condemn others. God's Word tells us that we should not judge others without first judging ourselves (Matthew 7:1-5). We may think that the choices we make are fine, but as we apply the Word of God, we also see our lives in the Light of Christ (John 8:12). Though we are not perfect, God may use our mistakes to make us stronger. Then we can testify of His forgiveness and grace, and continue faithfully in His will as sons and daughters of *the Most High God* (Genesis 14:20).

Of all the gifts (talents) and opportunities that God gives us, we can show our gratitude by using them to represent Christ. As we continue to grow in faith, our lives will reflect the joy of salvation. Therefore we must allow the Holy Spirit to lead us so we will not cause others to stumble, but rather to be encouraged and receive salvation (1 Corinthians 10:32-33).

God desires to have all of us (His children) with Him (1 Timothy 2:1-6). As we share our faith, others will come to know Him and receive Him because He is Lord and Savior of the world. *"[18]And Jesus came and spake unto them, saying, All power is given unto me in heaven and in earth. [19]Go ye therefore, and teach all nations, baptizing them in the name of the Father, and of the Son, and of the Holy Ghost; [20]Teaching them to observe all things whatsoever I have commanded you: and, lo, I am with you alway, even unto the end of the world. Amen"* (Matthew 28:18-20).

When I think about salvation, I immediately think about the love that God showed towards us when His only Son, Jesus Christ, died on the cross, was buried, and rose from the dead in victory. God sent Jesus to the world, and with this mission God Himself, through Jesus Christ who is fully God and fully man (John 14:7), experienced a physical birth, life, and death because of His love and compassion for us. At the cross, Christ paid the price for our sins, cleansing us of all guilt, shame, and condemnation so that we will not suffer the penalty of sin which is eternal death. Only Jesus, the Lamb of God, slain to redeem the world, is worthy to save us from death. Because of His sacrifice, we are free from sin, not free to sin. Therefore, we must not take Him for granted or try to justify certain sins for our personal pleasures.

After Jesus' resurrection and after being seen by several (1 Corinthians 15:1-8), before He ascended to Heaven and sat at the right hand of the Father (Mark 16:19), He promised to return for us (2 Peter 3:1-10). Until then, He prayed that God will send us the Spirit of Truth (the Holy Spirit, the Comforter) (John 14:16-17), who resides within us to guide us until He returns. As we go through the trials of life (John 16:33) we know that God is with us because the Spirit of the Lord dwells within us, and God, Jesus Christ, and the Holy Spirit are One (Matthew 28:19-20). Though they are One, they are also three individual Persons of the Godhead (Colossians 2:9; Matthew 28:19b).

We glorify God the Father, the Son, and the Holy Ghost when we tell others about Christ and how through Him we have everlasting life (John 3:16), for our God is the One and Only, True and Living God (1 Thessalonians 1:9). Therefore, we should be excited to share the Good News and let others know that Jesus Christ is alive and He is the only Way to receive *salvation* (John 14:6).

Salvation (divine deliverance from sin) is such a precious gift not meant to be contained, but instead, meant to be shared so the world will know that Christ lives, and His love and forgiveness is immeasurable. God looks beyond all our faults and failures, and our mistakes of the past, present, and future to see the Creation that He wants us to also see in ourselves. He has a plan for each of our lives (Jeremiah 29:11) that He wants us to fulfill right here on Earth—*to be a light for others*. With this in mind, I think about how Christ's incredible sacrifice touched and continues to touch so many lives, long after He gave His life for us on the cross. Our brand new life in Christ allows us freedom from condemnation (Romans 8:1) through the redeeming blood Christ shed for us.

Through Christ, you too can have a brand new life (2 Corinthians 6:17). No matter who you are, or what you have done, the love of Christ is strong enough to cleanse you of all unrighteousness. There is no greater love than the love of Christ (John 15:13). Romans 10:9,10 tells how to start a relationship with Him. Though you may continue to experience adverse situations or uncertainties, the Lord is with you every step of the way to see you through. He wants you to learn to trust Him, especially in times of trouble when life tends to produce the most hardships and distractions.

Just remember, this Earth is not our home. It is a temporary place where we can exercise our faith in God and look forward to being with Him eternally in Heaven. Until then, if we keep looking to God, following Christ, and submitting to the Holy Spirit, we will see that we can accomplish all things through Christ who gives us strength (Philippians 4:13). Personally, I cannot imagine life without Christ. That is why with thankfulness, I give God glory and praise for all He has done in my life, as I am blessed with opportunities to share my faith.

If you have not already accepted Jesus Christ as your Lord and Savior, I pray that you will allow Him to come into your heart and be your Lord and Savior today. If you are ready right now, then pray the following prayer with me:

"Dear Heavenly Father, I acknowledge You today as the One and Only, True and Living God, Creator of Heaven and Earth. I praise You and thank You for allowing Your only Son, Jesus Christ, to die for my sins so that I may have eternal life with You in Heaven. I confess that I am a sinner, and I am asking Jesus Christ to come into my heart and be

my Lord and Savior. I believe with all my heart that He died on the cross, was buried, and rose from the dead. Today, I submit my life as a living sacrifice to You. Thank You for allowing the Holy Spirit to come into my heart to lead, guide, and direct me all the days of my life. I love You and from this day forward You are my God. I pray this prayer in Your Son Jesus' Name. Amen."

To continue walking faithfully with Christ, set aside time to read God's Word (the Holy Bible), either from a printed or electronic version. <u>BLESSINGS IN BLOGS: LIVING EFFECTIVELY</u> references the King James Version. However, you may want to start with the New King James Version (NKJV) or New International Version (NIV) for a more contemporary translation. Connect with a Bible teaching church in your area for support as you grow spiritually in the Lord. Most of all, pray daily and stay encouraged so you may encourage others. Remember, we are saved to share our faith with others, so they may be saved to share their faith with others.

Comments | Share Your Faith

Now and Forever

ONE EVENING DURING my personal Bible study, an interesting thought came to mind. I realized that I had been limiting the scope of God's Word to *preparation for life on Earth.* I never thought of how it also applies to *preparation for eternal life with God.*

An eternal life with the Lord doesn't mean that we will have nothing to do but walk around Heaven in amazement. We will enjoy serving the Lord through eternity. How do we know? Because it is written in God's Word, *"³ . . . and his servants shall serve [worship] him: ⁴And they shall see his face; and his name shall be in their foreheads. ⁵. . . for the Lord God giveth them light: and they shall reign for ever and ever"* (Revelation 22:3-5).

We will be completely in awe of the Lord, totally in His service, worshipping, and praising our God forever (Psalm 34:1; Psalm 150:1). *"⁸ . . . and they rest not day and night, saying, Holy, holy, holy, Lord God Almighty, which was, and is, and is to come"* (Revelation 4:8).

When we study the Bible we learn that our lives are more complete with God. Generally, we focus on two main aspects: (1) our love for God and others, and (2) sharing the Gospel of Jesus Christ. Yet, with all the daily distractions, we sometimes fail to serve and worship God as we should. Studying the Bible allows us to give God our full attention, learn more about Him, and learn that He is worthy to be served throughout eternity. We learn that God loves to see us serve in His name while we are on Earth, and our efforts will be rewarded in Heaven. The reward is not a ticket to Heaven (Ephesians 2:8-9), but a reward for our faithful living. Christ said, *"And, behold, I come quickly; and my reward is with me, to give every man according as his work shall be"* (Revelation 22:12; Isaiah 40:10). Our works on Earth are a result of our love for God and others and our faith in following Christ Jesus. We serve not to be saved, but because we are saved by grace.

We would never know about the eternal blessings of God—the gift of salvation and the reward when Christ returns, if we never study God's Word. Studying the Bible is preparation for life now and forever because God's Word is forever. *"The grass withereth, the flower fadeth: but the word of our God shall stand for ever"* (Isaiah 40:8).

Comments | Now and Forever

From Point A to Point B

GENERALLY SPEAKING, WITH every new challenge we face on a daily basis, one of our greatest concerns is to move from point A to point B. Regardless of the glare that sometimes obscures our vision, or the winds that may blow our opportunities, God gives us the drive to make a *hole in one* on the course of life. *"It is God that girdeth me with strength, and maketh my way perfect"* (Psalm 18:32). Therefore, because we are called to be a light in this world (Isaiah 42:6), we must not allow our daily routines or choices to become the obstacles or sand traps that try to defeat our purpose. As long as we keep our focus on Christ (Hebrews 12:1,2), we will stay on course and clearly reach the mark we are destined to achieve according to God's plans.

Looking back several years ago, I can recall when God revealed a new direction in my life, a new journey for which He was preparing me for quite some time. I have had many opportunities over the years to write for the companies where I was employed, yet the inspiring words that God placed on my heart seemed to never get any further than my computer or loose leaf paper in a binder. I can remember waking up in the middle of the night, grabbing a sheet of paper and a pen to write the remnants of a dream. Likewise, throughout the day, I would try to memorize inspirational thoughts that crossed my mind until I was able to write them down. I wanted to hold on to the words to reference later or share with others. While my written thoughts soon became stacks of paper on my desk and files on my computer, I began to consider the possibility of one day compiling my notes to write a book. But because each day seemed to allow fewer hours than my life actually required, I chose to prioritize my previous obligations and daily responsibilities that included my family, ministry efforts, and employment. I didn't want to be selfish, so I ended up postponing my calling all together because at that time I thought it was just a personal interest or pastime.

The more I yielded to the distractions the more I postponed my calling. Still, it's funny that no matter how many times or how many ways I focused on other responsibilities, I would always come back to what God intended (Proverbs 20:24). So every now and then, I would continue jotting down the inspirational words that crossed my mind; but for the most part, I still allowed everything else to monopolize my time. After years of the same routine, I came to realize that because I didn't make the right choice to prioritize God's calling, I ended up well *over par*. I made several attempts to take a swing in the direction God was leading me, but I missed the mark because I wasn't focused on Him. Though God's plan will always prevail (Isaiah 55:11) I was holding up my blessing by not prioritizing His will (Numbers 14:26-34).

Then at the start of the year 2007, Pastor Calvin Hooper of Round Rock, Texas, author of <u>Walk the Walk: 8 Essentials for Living the Christian Life</u>, spoke of how seven is the Biblical number of completion (Genesis 2:1-3; 8:4). He challenged the congregation to move forward on whatever we believed that God was leading us to do that we put off over the years. The first thing that came to my mind was to finish writing and publishing a book that I started years ago. Though I was always able to use my writing abilities to fulfill my professional responsibilities, inspirational writing is my passion. It is something I enjoy because I learn from what God places on my heart to write and share with others. After years of writing my thoughts, I finally began to see writing as part of God's plan for my life.

From the moment we enter this world at birth, we are unaware of God, who we are, or our specific purpose in life. At first we begin to mature by trial and error until we are introduced to the Light of Jesus Christ, accept Him as our Lord and Savior, and learn that we can find direction in God's Word (Psalm 119:105) through the Holy Spirit. From that point on, what we do is by choice because we have been enlightened and the Holy Spirit is within us. Though we know right from wrong, we are at times challenged by our human nature, testing our commitment to walk the path God has placed before us as we decide to pursue our will or the will of God. Apostle Paul describes the battle of man's will by admitting that *what he should do he does not, yet he does what he knows he should not do* (Romans 7:15). This statement seems to be the self-willed tendency of all humanity[3]. Yet regardless of our selfishness, God loves us and restores us to a right relationship with Him through our faith in Jesus Christ.

I don't always understand the reason why some things happen now, later, or not at all; but I know God has a perfect plan and purpose for all His Creation. Our part in His plan is to trust Him and follow His lead to get from point A to point B.

There is a saying that stands true: *"timing is everything."* Though more importantly, God's timing is perfect. Three years later I received confirmation to move forward with publishing my first book when Pastor Joe Champion of Georgetown, Texas encouraged the congregation to actively reach for what we are called by God to accomplish. He expressed how his purpose as the pastor of the church would not be fulfilled if he didn't encourage the people of God to follow where God is leading them.

God has a purpose for every life He created, a very essential part of His Master Plan. He even provides direction in His Holy Word so we will know how to fulfill our calling. All we have to do is trust Him and follow. When we commit to follow Christ without turning to the left or to the right (Proverbs 4:27), we are more committed to fulfill God's perfect plan in His perfect time.

Comments | From Point A to Point B

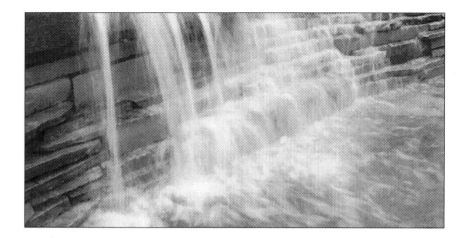

The Absolute Fulfillment of Life

Unconditional love, commitment, and obedience are three vital attributes of a believer in Christ. Faith, in particular, encompasses these attributes, allowing believers to look beyond any circumstance or situation and press forward to achieve the specific purpose for which they are called by God (Philippians 3:14). Those who allow the Holy Spirit to help them mature in these and other spiritual attributes gain confidence and strength to accomplish all things through Christ (Philippians 4:13).

God has a purpose and a plan for every individual and He has given each of us provisions to complete every task in the process. He also allows us to take part in supporting the vision of spiritual leaders whom He has placed in charge of leading and ministering to the church and the community. This does not mean that we should neglect the opportunities God gives us individually. Finding the ultimate balance between serving God and others, while fulfilling our God-given purpose is what I call *"the absolute fulfillment of life."* When our purpose is to please God, we find the energy and strength to accomplish all that He has called us to achieve.

Serving in the church and thus serving others is essential (Galatians 6:10; Romans 12:10-13) to help further the kingdom of God. He has given each of us talents that we can use to support the development of the church (1 Corinthians 12:4-14;27-31); however, we are responsible for taking care of our families and our physical body as well. Therefore, we must balance our responsibilities to be most effective. This balance creates a steady flow of intertwining streams of life directed by God.

God never intended for us to over extend ourselves in any particular task. If we follow His lead we will find time to do all that we are called to do, including time to rest. *"And God blessed the seventh day, and sanctified[5] it: because that in it he had rested from all his work which God created and made"* (Genesis 2:3). Certainly, we ought to look to God because He is our Creator (Ephesians 3:9). He knows the exact purpose for which He created us, and He will help us become victorious in our efforts as we keep Him first above all that we hope to achieve.

Yet, some people attribute a fulfilling life to one that focuses on reaching "their goals" in the timeframe "they expect." This outlook is based on socially accepted expectations and pressures. It is in the heart of the unsaved[7] and the mind of the carnal believer, still struggling with completely submitting his or her life to God. Both individuals have succumbed to the deception of the world—the belief that they are in control; however, this mindset will eventually lead to self-destruction.

Individuals who fall into this belief sometimes choose to focus every effort on living a lifestyle above their means. Consequently, with no concern for their future, they may end up broke and alone (Luke 15:11-16). As a result, they feel like they lost everything, not realizing that they had all that they really needed. Without God, all accolades and possessions are only temporary. They do not define a person's life and they certainly do not please God. Luke 12:15 *reminds us that our lives do not consist of the things that we possess.*

Believers who achieve balance in their lives through the grace of God, ultimately reach a point where they can enjoy the fruits of their efforts (Psalm 128:1,2). This is so, because their focus is not on what everyone expects of them, but where God is leading them. They choose not to worry about anything, because the Heavenly Father already knows what they need (Matthew 6:31-32). Instead, they seek God first above all else (Matthew 6:33), knowing that God will always provide.

These individuals receive the favor of God because they know and acknowledge God through worship and praise for all that He has done. Their appreciation isn't merely a notable gesture or out of religious obligation; but rather, sincere and true in response to the Holy Spirit. They know that God is their life and that He supplies all that they need (Philippians 4:19).

What sets these individuals apart is their will to move from self-will to God's will. When we come into this world, we begin to learn from the people in our lives, adapt to our environment, and draw information from various technical devices that compete for our attention. Until we are introduced to a life in Christ, we become naturally inclined to focus on the advances of the world because of our sinful nature. All things considered, we will either continue striving for a life of fulfillment or we will live the absolute fulfillment of life through Christ Jesus.

Comments | The Absolute Fulfillment of Life

MONDAY, NOVEMBER 8, 7:20 P.M.

Today

TODAY IS A gift from God, a portrait of possibilities, framed and ready to display for our personal enjoyment. It is a masterpiece that depicts the passion of God (the Artist), drawing admirers to participate in an amazing design. Of course every detail He planned and purposed because He is the Creator of Heaven and Earth (Genesis 1:1).

Every element of this design has a specific purpose. There are elements that are always present and those that are newly introduced. The elements that are prevalent identify His Work. These are the elements we generally recognize and enjoy no matter what, such as the sun that provides light, warmth, and a calming sense of peace that He is always with us (Matthew 28:20); the trees that show us how to stand strong regardless of our circumstances; and the brilliant sky that reminds us of the brighter side of life, even when we feel blue. These are constants that keep everything in perspective if we choose to see them and hold on to them for the beauty they possess. As for the elements of surprise, we must always be willing and ready to learn something new every day.

I must admit, I haven't always approached each day with joy regardless of what was going on or about to happen. I automatically responded with the way each situation made me feel and I would sometimes take quite a while to remember the most important element of the day—the fact that God is and will always be in complete control. This means that every day is an incredible gift of beauty designed just the way God planned (Psalm 118:24).

Comments | Today

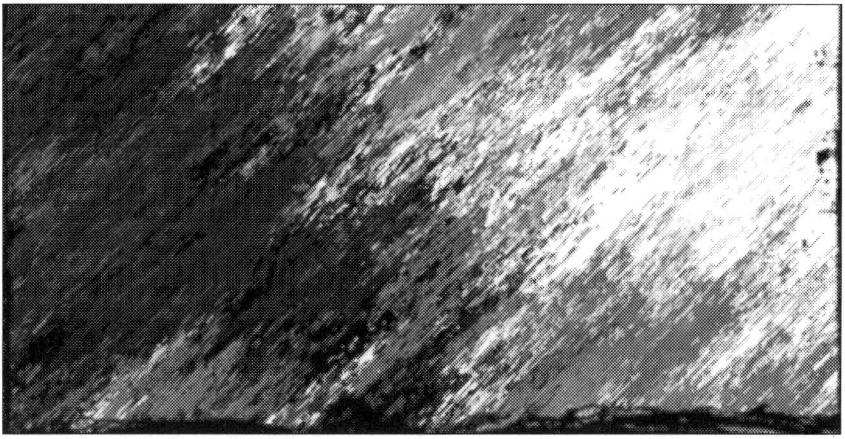

SATURDAY, NOVEMBER 13, 11:45 A.M.

Be a Light

SOMETIMES THE MOST challenging part of being a Christian is to be a light in this ever-changing world, to *stand firm in the faith* (1 Corinthians 16:13) and represent Jesus Christ in the midst of the ungodly. We should stand not haughtily above and certainly not below what is pleasing to God, but rather in a way that will demonstrate our faith and extend the Light of Christ.

During His powerful sermon known as the Sermon on the Mount, Jesus said, "[14]*Ye are the light of the world. A city that is set on a hill cannot be hid.* [15]*Neither do men light a candle, and put it under a bushel, but on a candlestick; and it giveth light unto all that are in the house.* [16]*Let your light so shine before men, that they may see your good works, and glorify your Father which is in heaven*" (Matthew 5:14-16).

When we find ourselves in the midst of the unsaved[7] at work, school, and even among some of our family members, we may at times feel out of place because we prefer not to participate in activities that compromise our spiritual life. Still, we must never become arrogant because we all have victories to achieve. Nor should we step out of the Light of Jesus

Christ (John 9:5) and confuse the unsaved[7] while trying to reach out to them. Instead, we must maintain a balance so not to make others back away from the Light of Christ that is within us.

To hold up the Light of Christ among the unsaved[7], the Holy Spirit allows us to recall God's Word, and He helps us follow the principles as we represent Christ. In other words, our goal is to not only share the love of Christ by referencing the Word of God in our conversations as God presents the opportunity, but also to allow the Word of God to help us take the right approach (Philippians 2:13-16). Thus, whenever God gives us the opportunity to be His voice, we must speak according to God's will to represent Christ effectively. *"For the Word of God is quick [living], and powerful, and sharper than any two-edged sword, piercing even to the dividing asunder of soul and spirit, and of the joints and marrow, and is a discerner of the thoughts and intents of the heart"* (Hebrews 4:12).

In his sermon titled "Behold, The Beauty of Unity," Elder William R. Thicklin of Kansas City, Kansas reminds us that *"When we observe the scripture that is laid bare before us, we must understand that God is giving us a formula. If we acknowledge the formula, we can only be successful in achieving its desired end."* The Word of God is our guide to help us accomplish what God has called us to do.

As ambassadors for Christ (2 Corinthians 5:20-21), we must follow His commitment to fulfill the will of God (John 9:4), *"For God sent not his Son into the world to condemn the world; but that the world through him might be saved"* (John 3:17). Therefore, we cannot think too highly of ourselves (Romans 12:3) so not to take on the seductive character of pride (Proverbs 8:13). Nor should we yield to conformity (Romans 12:2) and take part in the deeds of darkness—never making the difference God intended.

When we as Christians received the Light of Christ, we experienced an extraordinary change. For the first time in our lives, we saw ourselves for who we really are, because the Light revealed our imperfections, so much so that we desired to be changed (2 Corinthians 5:17). As we continue in this new life, we realize through our tests and trials, we have much to learn. Nevertheless, with Christ Jesus, the grace of God sustains us while we improve our position on the learning curve of spiritual maturity.

In this world, we will experience many situations that require extra attention and effort. It is up to us to further our spiritual strength through studying the Word of God so we will be a light that shines brilliantly for Christ.

Comments | Be a Light

THURSDAY, NOVEMBER 25, 9:00 P.M.

"The Remedy"

WHETHER BATTLING A cold or just feeling down, one of the best remedies is to simply say *"Thank You God!"* for the life He has given through His Son Jesus Christ. Thankfulness is a remedy with unlimited doses. You can have as much as you want and as often as you choose without any conflicting side effects. It is easy to dispense and goes well with a loving spirit and a grateful heart. Gratitude is a reminder that God is the source of our strength and the light of our lives, for we cannot live without Him. When we focus on God our situations are not as significant. That's why our spirit is lifted when we come into His presence giving thanks. *"Enter into his gates with thanksgiving, and into his courts with praise: be thankful unto him, and bless his name. For the Lord is good; his mercy is everlasting; and his truth endureth to all generations"* (Psalm 100:4).

Various forms of the word thanks, such as the words *thanksgiving* and *thankworthy*, are listed in the Bible more than 100 times, which demonstrates the importance of gratitude towards God. Each instance of the word is provided in the list that follows. *"Thanks"* is a powerful word that contributes tremendously to our well-being and reminds us that we are blessed. *"In every thing give thanks: for this is the will of God in Christ Jesus . . ."* (1 Thessalonians 5:18).

Genesis 7:12 (twice), 13, 15; 22:29 (5 times)

2 Samuel 22:50 (1 time)

I Chronicles 16:8, 24, 27, 35, 41; 25:3; 31:2 (7 times)

Ezra 3:11 (1 time)

Nehemiah 11:17; 12:8, 24, 27, 31, 38, 40, 46 (8 times)

Psalm 6:5; 18:49; 26:7; 30:4, 12; 35:18; 50:14; 69:30; 75:1 (twice); 79:13; 92:1; 95:2; 97:12; 100:4; 105:1; 106:1, 47; 107:1, 22; 116:17; 118:1, 29; 199:62; 122:4; 136:1, 2, 3, 26; 140:13; 147:7 (31 times)

Isaiah 51:3 (1 time)

Jeremiah 30:19 (1 time)

Daniel 6:10 (1 time)

Amos 4:5 (1 time)

Jonah 2:9 (1 time)

Matthew 15:36; 26:27 (2 times)

Mark 8:6; 14:23 (2 times)

Luke 2:38; 17:16; 22:17, 19 (4 times)

John 6:11, 23 (2 times)

Acts 27:35 (1 time)

Romans 14:6; 16:4 (2 times)

1 Corinthians 10:30; 11:24; 14:16, 17; 15:57 (5 times)

2 Corinthians 1:11; 2:14; 4:15; 8:16; 9:11, 12; 9:15 (7 times)

Ephesians 1:16; 5:4, 20 (3 times)

Philippians 4:6 (1 time)

Colossians 1:3, 12; 2:7; 3:17; 4:2 (5 times)

1 Thessalonians 1:2; 3:9; 5:18 (3 times)

2 Thessalonians 2:13 (1 time)

1 Timothy 2:1; 4:3, 4 (3 times)

Philemon 13:15 (1 time)

1 Peter 2:19 (1 time)

Revelation 4:9, 11; 7:12; 11:17 (4 times)

Comments | The Remedy

WINTER SECTION

The Opportunity No One Wants, But Everyone Needs

ADVERSITY IS ACTUALLY an opportunity. Yet, it is a common part of life that no one wants to experience since it comes without warning and seems to hang around until another instance shows up.

While experiencing adversity, in an attempt to improve your situation as quickly as possible you may try to devise a plan. Then, as you lean on *your* expectations the situation tends to hang around a little while longer. Jesus said that we will find peace in Him, regardless of the battles we face because He already achieved for us a victorious win. He told His disciples that they will have trouble in this world, but don't worry because He has overcome the world (John 16:33).

Without trials, we would never have the opportunity to practice what we learn from our previous challenging experiences. Regardless of the situation, our response will definitely reveal where we are in our relationship with Christ. I believe that is why God's response to our prayers is sometimes *yes, no,* or *wait.* When we patiently wait, our strength is renewed for the journey (Isaiah 40:31).

By experiencing more of life's ups and particularly downs, we have the opportunity to grow closer to God. As we spiritually mature, and learn not to be disappointed or angry with God, we are more ready to accept His decisions and trust that He knows what's best. Of course He knows because He created us and has given His promise written in the Holy Bible in Deuteronomy 31:6 and Hebrews 13:5b, which tells us that He will never leave or forsake us.

Therefore, it's time to stop doubting God or complaining about His will. It's time to commit to a trusting relationship with God through Christ Jesus, our Lord and Savior, the Mediator between God and humanity[3]. Like me, you may think you have, but when you look back at how you felt or how you reacted to certain unfavorable situations you may think differently.

At first it may be difficult to see adversity as an opportunity for spiritual growth. It's just something you have to learn with experience. The more you come to know God through His Word and through your situations, the more you learn to trust Him and experience the peace that goes far beyond what you could ever comprehend (Philippians 4:7; Proverbs 3:5,6). Adversity is the opportunity no one wants but everyone needs. This is the kind of opportunity that really makes you strong. This is what the Apostle Paul referred to in 2 Corinthians 12:10 when he said, *"Therefore I take pleasure in infirmities, in reproaches, in necessities, in persecutions, in distresses for Christ's sake: for when I am weak, then am I strong."*

Comments | The Opportunity No One Wants, But Everyone Needs

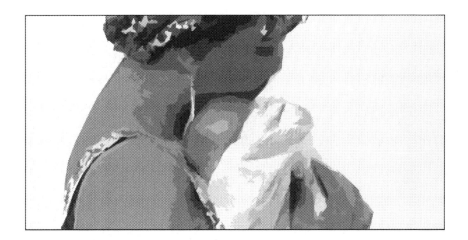

WEDNESDAY, DECEMBER 9, 6:15 P.M.

Growing Closer to God

EVERY NOW AND then I think about the times when I was disappointed with God because certain events in my life turned out so different from my expectations. Knowing that God is in control of everything, I couldn't understand why He allowed these situations to happen. For instance, many years ago, my husband and I prayed and asked God to heal our infant son who was born with a liver disease. After having a miscarriage earlier that same year, this beautiful, premature baby boy was supposed to be the miracle we desperately needed. He was very ill, but we knew that God could heal him because *nothing is too hard for the Lord* (Genesis 18:14). My husband and I were young at the time in age as well as in faith. However, we trusted God to heal our son because there was nothing that we could do on our own to save him (Matthew 19:26; Luke 1:37). Still, with all our prayers and the prayers of family and friends, our son went home to be with the Lord anyway.

As I look back, this was the most devastating, spiritually challenging time of our lives. Each of us handled the pain of our loss in our own way. My husband seemed to focus on work while I needed to talk about what happened because it seemed so unfair. I just couldn't get over the fact that God had given us this beautiful little life that was gone before we got to know him.

The first and most natural response parents may have when they lose a young child is to blame God for leaving them with empty arms. Though not even for a moment will God leave or forsake us, especially in a time of sorrow. Instead, He fills the void with compassion and comfort (2 Corinthians 1:3) because He loves us.

"So, why didn't God save our child?" The answer is, *"He did."* He gave him a brand new life without having to suffer from the illness that attacked him when he entered this life. In general, when we hear about devastating tragedies our hearts ache over the lives that *seem to expire too soon.* Nevertheless, though God has the power to heal, He also has a plan for every life that comes into this world. Some of us require more time to fulfill our purpose in life while others will only need a short while.

Though this was a very trying time for us, it was also the greatest demonstration of God's love as He held us up and healed the wounds from our loss. Through it all, God gave us the strength to continue our journey knowing that our son is alive and well in the arms of our Heavenly Father.

As the years passed by, my husband and I continued learning to trust God in every aspect of our lives, including our family, jobs, and finances. Through the spoken Word of God and our personal Bible study, we learned to tithe (See March 12, "About Tithing"). Tithing allowed us to give back to God one tenth of our income (our increase) in obedience to His Word (Hebrews 7:4-9) to demonstrate that nothing in this world is more important than God. But soon after we started tithing we lost our jobs around the same time due to an economic downturn. Though I knew that God would never let us down, I was disappointed and a little worried—especially since we had an eight year old son and a baby daughter at the time.

While believing what the Lord promised in John 14:14, *"If you ask anything in my name, I will do it,"* we prayed that God would move on our situation and bring us through this very uncertain time. What I failed to realize is that God's response is according to His will and according to His plan, in His time and for His glory. *"Thou art worthy, O Lord, to receive glory and honour and power: for thou hast created all things, and for thy pleasure they are and were created"* (Revelation 4:11).

Because of God's sovereignty, He will do whatever we ask that is *"in His will."* He is our Creator and He knows exactly how He wants everything to work together for good (Romans 8:28). Moreover, we are the children of God (John 1:12; 1 John 3:1,2) and therefore should follow His lead. As the perfect parent, God will never spoil us (His children) or give us the authority to tell Him when and how to respond. He is our Heavenly Father and like any loving parent, He knows what is best and expects His children to trust Him (Proverbs 3:5,6).

God's love for His children is genuine, a love like no other. He demonstrates His love for us daily, especially in the most trying situations—tests of faith that give us the opportunity to prioritize His will. I believe that our faith is tested from time to time so we will know whether we truly love God as much as we claim. Over the years, the more my husband and I learn about being in God's will, the more we grow in our relationship with Christ, and with each other.

God gave us peace in knowing that there is a bigger picture—*a Masterpiece* in the making. As a result, my husband and I became instruments of encouragement for others who have experienced some of the same disappointments (2 Corinthians 1:4). Through it all, we learned that when our hearts are tested by what we don't readily understand, in time God will reveal the fulfillment of His plan. Think of it this way: every obstacle presents greater opportunities to grow closer to God.

Comments | Growing Closer to God

What Really Matters

WHETHER OR NOT you receive thanks for what you have done, or receive an apology for what someone else has done to you, it doesn't really matter. When others overlook your kind gestures or chose not to show remorse for their wrong doings towards you, for your sake, let it go. Your kindness is an expression of thanks to God (Colossians 3:17), and your forgiveness towards them demonstrates gratitude for God's forgiveness towards you (Ephesians 4:32; Colossians 3:13.) Don't make the issue any bigger than it really is by allowing it to distract you from what God expects you to do. As Christians, we receive a much higher honor when we receive God's favor. We receive the favor of God in the blessings He has given and through His mercy and grace.

Not everyone cares about the same things, and everyone's choices are not determined from the same perspective. So why stress over something that you have no control over? Every individual is only responsible for his or her actions. Therefore, pray and ask God to give you peace so you won't give power to that which doesn't really matter. Peace in the matter is not about letting others get the best of you. Christ certainly had good reason to fight back for the way He was treated, but He chose to stay focused on what God expected of Him. Not everyone will treat you the way they should, or the way you expect. Besides, you really can't force them because it's their choice. The best you can do is treat others with the love and respect you would like to receive, rather than how you feel about them or the matter. *"And as ye would that men should do to you, do ye also to them likewise"* (Luke 6:31). If you choose to respond by how you feel, you may later regret your choice.

What REALLY matters to me is that God is pleased in my efforts, *". . . to do good and to communicate forget not: for with such sacrifices God is well pleased"* (Hebrews 13:16). Even if whatever I do doesn't *seem* to make a difference at the time, or if I have to sacrifice time from what I want to do in order to do what God is calling me to do, God matters the most because He comes first.

Just as we seek the blessings of God, we must seek to do well by others in order to bless God (Psalm 34:1), regardless of how others respond (Matthew 7:12). Pleasing God is all that really matters *"because greater is he that is in you, than he that is in the world"* (1 John 4:4b).

Comments | What Really Matters

Choices

EVERY DAY BRINGS new choices—what to do, what to think, and what to say. Some are more difficult than others, especially the ones we least expect. For the most part, choices are basically unavoidable because at some point they have to be made.

Everyone has choices to make in life and typically every choice is made according to the personality and preferences of the one who is making the decision. However, the best results come from choices that are based on God's Word and the prompting of the Holy Spirit. God will not honor what He has not authorized.

God gives each of us the right to make our own decisions, even though He already knows what we will do. He created us and knows us personally (Psalm 139:1-4) like parents know their own children. He wants what's best for us, but loves us enough to let us make our own decisions so we will learn from our experiences.

Every now and then the choices we make may cause us to stumble and sometimes lose our way. Consequently, we have the choice to remain lost or repent (Matthew 4:17) and return to our Father's love (Luke 15:11-32).

If we choose not to return, we struggle in self-pity or pride (Proverbs 16:18; James 4:6) and forego the blessings He is willing to provide in our obedience.

The Lord will guide us even in the midst of our troubles (Psalm 138:7). God has the power to turn our downfalls into victories for our good and for His glory. Though we may have to accept a few wounds from the battle, we will endure because we know that *all things work out for good to them that love God and are called according to His purpose* (Romans 8:28).

Sometimes having a choice is not as overwhelming when it is about something we are familiar with, such as selecting an item on a menu or shoes from our closet. When choices are unfamiliar or full of uncertainties, they tend to present a challenge for the decision-maker—especially with choices that are more important than others. They can make you feel pretty good about yourself *if* the right choice is made, or they can leave you feeling divided if they involve something or someone you care about. No matter how big or small, simple or complicated, the best decisions are made with the guidance of the Lord (Psalm 25:9). Choices not only affect your present and future, but more importantly, your eternal life. The choice to invite Jesus Christ into your heart as your Lord and Savior is more than a life changing experience. It marks the beginning of a brand new life in Christ (2 Corinthians 5:17).

For just a moment, right where you are, take a glance at whatever light source is available in your view—perhaps a lamp, a candle, or a ray of sunshine. Now close your eyes for just a second. Even when you take your eyes off the light it still shines just as brightly. Generally, it will not turn itself off. It is still there because it has a specific purpose. Regardless of whether you chose to see it or not, its purpose is still fulfilled whether or not you are watching. Likewise, regardless of whether you accept or reject Christ as your Lord and Savior, He will forever be King of Kings and Lord of Lords. He is and will always be the Light of the world (John 9:5); and He is ready to come into your heart if you allow Him (Revelation 3:20). He wants you to have an abundant life (John 10:10) that will last forever (John 6:27). He is the only One who can bring you into a right relationship with God by accepting His gift of salvation—eternal life in Christ (John 4:14).

To accept the gift of salvation, we must be born again. *"Jesus said, Verily, verily* [truly], *I say unto thee, Except a man [a human being] be born again, he cannot see the kingdom of God"* (John 3:3). This birth is of water and spirit, not of flesh as when we entered into the world (John 3:5,6). When we are born again, we become children of God (Romans 8:16,17), co-heirs to His kingdom. *". . . Whosoever shall not receive the kingdom of God as a little child, he shall not enter therein"* (Mark 10:15). Though some people may come to know Christ in their adult life, all believers enter into the family of God as a newborn, maturing spiritually, growing in grace and knowledge of the Lord (2 Peter 3:18).

Choose to receive the Lord Jesus Christ by first admitting that you are a sinner—as with all humans when we come into the world (Psalm 51:5; Romans 3:23; Isaiah 53:6). Believe that Jesus Christ is the Son of God (Mark 1:11; 2 Peter 1:17,18; Matthew 27:43) and that He is the only way for you to come into a right relationship with God our Heavenly Father (John 14:6). Believe that only Jesus Christ can forgive your sins (Mark 2:7-12; John 8:24,58) through the sacrificial blood that He shed when He was crucified (Matthew 27:11-66). With all considered, when you verbally confess the Lord Jesus Christ, and believe in your heart that He died on the cross, was buried, and rose from the dead on the third day, you are saved[5] (Romans 10:9,10; 1 Corinthians 15:1-4; Luke 24:46,47).

This declaration of your faith along with water baptism identifies you with the death, burial, and resurrection of Christ (Romans 6:3,4). It is a testimony to others that Jesus Christ is now Lord and Savior of your life. You are a new creation in Christ (2 Corinthians 5:17), and as a new creation you have chosen to repent (Acts 2:38); that is, turn away from your previous ways of living to live a life that is pleasing to God (Romans 6:18).

Through His sacrifice, Jesus demonstrated the kind of love that no one could ever express. His love creates a relationship that connects us to God the Father, God the Son, and God the Holy Spirit.

"⁷For there are three that bear record in heaven, the Father, the Word [Jesus Christ], and the Holy Ghost [Holy Spirit]: and these three are one [united]. ¹¹And this is the record, that God hath given to us eternal life, and this life is in his Son. ¹²He that hath the Son hath life; and he that hath not the Son of God hath not life. ¹³These things have I written unto you that believe on the name of the Son of God; that ye may know that ye have eternal life, and that ye may believe on the name of the Son of God" (1 John 5:7, 11-13).

If you have chosen to receive salvation, you will have a new path of life. This path will lead you on a journey of experiences that are challenging yet absolutely satisfying as you learn to follow Christ and walk out God's plan for your life. Commit to be the person God created and called you to be. "*Serve the Lord with gladness*" (Psalm 100:2a) so that others may also come to know Him through your life. "*. . . be thou an example of the believers, in word, in conversation, in charity, in spirit, in faith, in purity"* (1 Timothy 4:12*).*

God allows us to *choose whom we will serve* (Joshua 24:15). When we choose to serve Christ we choose Life and receive the gift of salvation. If you haven't accepted this priceless gift then choose Christ today while you still have the opportunity. No one knows when our Savior will return (Matthew 24:42).

"³¹When the Son of man shall come in his glory, and all the holy angels with him, then shall he sit upon the throne of his glory: ³²And before him shall be gathered all nations: and he shall separate them one from another, as a shepherd divideth his sheep from the goats: ³³And he shall set the sheep on his right hand, but the goats on the left. ³⁴Then shall the King say unto them on his right hand, Come, ye blessed of my Father, inherit the kingdom prepared for you from the foundation of the world:" (Matthew 25:31-34).

Comments | Choices

Everlasting Peace and Incredible Joy

"⁸And there were in the same country shepherds abiding in the field, keeping watch over their flock by night. ⁹And, lo, the angel of the Lord came upon them, and the glory of the Lord shone round about them: and they were sore afraid. ¹⁰And the angel said unto them, Fear not: for, behold, I bring you good tidings of great joy, which shall be to all people. ¹¹For unto you is born this day in the city of David a Savior, which is Christ the Lord. ¹²And this shall be a sign unto you; Ye shall find the babe wrapped in swaddling clothes, lying in a manger. ¹³And suddenly there was with the angel a multitude of heavenly host praising God, and saying, ¹⁴Glory to God in the highest and on earth peace, good will toward men. ²¹And when eight days were accomplished for the circumcising of the child, his name was called JESUS...." (Luke 2:8-14; 21).

JESUS CHRIST IS the pinnacle of perfection, the only perfect man that walked the Earth. No one else can compare, though we strive for the perfection of Christ in order to live a life pleasing to God our Heavenly Father. God's Word specifically tells us, *"Be ye therefore perfect, even as your Father which is in heaven is perfect"* (Matthew 5:48). Christ is our perfect example (1 Timothy 1:16).

Living a righteous life, a life right by God, is a lifestyle that we learn to develop as we mature in our relationship with Christ. From the start when we were created by God, we were equipped to carry out His will as He carefully designed each individual prior to our physical birth (Jeremiah 1:5). But while we physically mature, we must choose to refrain from worldly distractions and keep our eyes focused on Jesus Christ our Lord and Savior (Hebrews 12:1,2).

The unsaved[7] and even some of the saved[5], have yet to make Christ the center of their lives. Christ is not their focus because they can't really see how He would make a difference in their current situations. Those who don't believe are deceived and those who believe but are uncertain lack faith. All the while, both are missing out on the everlasting peace and the incredible joy they can only experience through a committed relationship with Christ. It's unfortunate that so many people miss out while trying to figure out life on their own. A strong relationship with Christ allows us to withstand any obstacle, and excel in any opportunities that otherwise seem impossible.

Most people know about Jesus' birth, death, burial, and resurrection through Christmas and Easter (Resurrection Day). Basically, they know Him by these nationally recognized holidays rather than the purpose His life served and the life His love provided. Thus, the more the world focuses on the celebration, with little or no regard to the Savior, the more lives remain lost or uncommitted. Though we who are saved[5] may wear scars from our battles, we are victorious in the end through our Lord Christ Jesus. He is the Light of the world. He is our everlasting peace and incredible joy.

Comments | Everlasting Peace and Incredible Joy

God's Word in Prayer: Divine Intervention

THE POWER OF prayer is experienced not only as a result of praying, but also in the midst of the prayer. No matter how long you have been saved[5], God speaks through those who have a sincere heart, as you come into His presence fully trusting Him. *". . . , take no thought how or what ye shall speak: for it shall be given you in the same hour what ye shall speak. For it is not ye that speak, but the Spirit of your Father which speaketh in you"* (Matthew 10:19-20). You don't have to worry about what to say or how to say it because the Lord will teach you (Exodus 4:10-12).

One evening I received a phone call from a friend I hadn't heard from in years. The beginning of our conversation was spent catching up on the years that had gone by, though in her voice I could tell that something was troubling her. For years she had been going through many trying times, and each time we talked, there was always a concern.

As with the other times when she was overwhelmed, she would ask me to pray for her, and I would before the end of the phone call. But this particular time when she asked, I felt the need to try something different. Because she was in a similar situation as years ago, devastated from unemployment, I responded this time by asking her to lead the prayer while I pray silently with her by phone. I was hoping God would move on her situation once and for all by having her make a personal request of God directly from her voice.

Initially she hesitated and said that she couldn't pray very well. So I reminded her that prayer is not about giving an elaborate speech for others who are listening to commend. Prayer is an honest communication with God that expresses trust and agreement with His will. Allowing her to lead the prayer placed her right in the position to stay focused on God. Finally, she began to speak with Him one to One.

Experiencing the power of such an earnest prayer during this divine intervention was a testimony of her willingness to trust God and my willingness to let God have His way. Her prayer not only allowed her voice to be heard by God but also allowed her to use God's Words from the Holy Bible while speaking to Him, something she never thought she could do. In such an enlightening moment the Holy Spirit enable her to speak the essence of God's Word in her prayer while using everyday language—pure and simple from the heart. Jesus said, *"Blessed are the pure in heart: for they shall see God"* (Matthew 5:8). She didn't realize it because she was still fairly new in her walk with Christ and hadn't spent much time studying God's Word to recognize how it applied. The Scriptures that her prayer referenced were not necessarily verbatim, but the essence of God's Word was truly present. Her prayer was powerful and sincere from the depths of her heart as she invited God into every area of her life.

Incorporating God's Word in our prayers is an effective way to communicate with God because we are letting Him know that we believe what He has promised. Prayer brings us closer to God as He gives each of us His undivided attention whenever we call on Him (Psalm 65:2). In response, I immediately began to encourage my friend to continue praying and reading God's Word, and soon she will be more familiar with the Scriptures to include in her prayer. Before we ended our phone conversation, I promised her that I would find the Scriptures that I heard her mention in prayer and send them to her so she could refer to them for future reference.

Comments | God's Word in Prayer: Divine Intervention

God's Word in Prayer: Scriptures, Part 1

AFTER MY FRIEND prayed, I expressed how her prayer was so heartfelt and that her words lined up beautifully with the Word of God. Being a young believer in Christ, she didn't realize that what she said actually referenced several Scriptures of the Bible. I believe that our prayers are more effective when we reference God's Word. With the help of the Holy Spirit, she prayed with sincerity and faith that God would hear her prayer.

For confidentiality, I will refrain from including direct quotes from her prayer, and instead provide a brief description of her prayer in bold print, followed by the Scriptures I believe applied. I hope to express how, with the help of the Holy Spirit, a believer that is uncomfortable praying aloud can pray without fear of what to say or how to say it, regardless of his or her level of faith or spiritual maturity. Prayer is an intimate and purposeful conversation that comes from the believer's heart where God has sent the Spirit of His Son (Galatians 4:6). When we pray with sincerity of heart (Luke 6:45) in reverence to God, we participate in a conversation with God through the Holy Spirit. Prayer based on God's Word allows us to connect with God and know that He is listening. It is a powerful experience that provides a sense of peace in the midst of any situation.

My friend started her prayer by humbly acknowledging that God is her Heavenly Father and Lord of her life. When we come to God with our requests, we must pray in adoration of God before we express our concerns.

> *"10Wherefore David blessed the Lord before all the congregation: and David said, Blessed be thou, Lord God of Israel our father, for ever and ever. 11Thine, O Lord, is the greatness, and the power, and the glory, and the victory, and the majesty: for all that is in the heaven and in the earth is thine; thine is the kingdom, O Lord, and thou art exalted as head above all. 12Both riches and honour come of thee, and thou reignest over all; and in thine hand is power and might; and in thine hand it is to make great, and to give strength unto all. 13Now therefore, our God, we thank thee, and praise thy glorious name"* (1 Chronicles 29:10-13).

As believers in Christ, we must pray in spirit and in truth (John 4:24), trusting God who knows what we need even before we ask (Matthew 6:8b).

She continued her prayer by repeating portions of the Lord's Prayer. Referencing "The Lord's Prayer," also known as "The Model Prayer," is an effective way of acknowledging and honoring the Lord. The Lord's Prayer appears in two forms in the Holy Bible. The following is the Lord's Prayer as it occurs in the Gospel of Matthew in the Sermon on the Mount.

> *"9After this manner therefore pray ye: Our Father which art in heaven, Hallowed be thy name. 10Thy kingdom come. Thy*

will be done in earth, as it is in heaven. [11]Give us this day our daily bread. [12]And forgive us our debts, as we forgive our debtors. [13]And lead us not into temptation, but deliver us from evil: For thine is the kingdom, and the power, and the glory, for ever. Amen" (Matthew 6:9-13).

The following is The Lord's Prayer as it occurs in the Gospel of Luke when one of Jesus' disciples asked Him to teach them to pray as John also taught His disciples.

"[2]And he said unto them, When ye pray, say, Our Father which art in heaven, Hallowed be thy name. Thy kingdom come. Thy will be done, as in heaven, so in earth. [3]Give us day by day our daily bread. [4]And forgive us our sins; for we also forgive every one that is indebted to us. And lead us not into temptation; but deliver us from evil" (Luke 11:2-4).

She also expressed that she knows that God loves her and cares for her, as He demonstrated in several situations. Prayer is our opportunity to acknowledge that we know God cares for us. He is truly concerned about us and He will take care of us. *"Casting all your care upon him; for he careth for you"* (1 Peter 5:7).

With remorse, she admitted her mistakes to God as she asked for His forgiveness. We all have made mistakes in life (Romans 3:23). As we pray and confess our sins with sincerity, through God's grace we are forgiven and our sins are no longer remembered (Isaiah 43:25). Through God's mercy we are brought back into a right relationship with Christ. *"If we confess our sins, he is faithful and just to forgive us our sins, and to cleanse us from all unrighteousness"* (1 John 1:9).

Hebrews 9:22 tells us that *". . . without [the] shedding of blood [there] is no remission [forgiveness of sin],"* which is why we can only be forgiven through the precious blood of Jesus Christ. The blood of Christ is the only blood worthy to be sacrificed to make us right with God. *"For Christ also hath once suffered for sins, the just for the unjust, that he might bring us to God"* (1 Peter 3:18a). *"In whom we have redemption through his [Jesus'] blood, the forgiveness of sins, according to the riches of his [God's] grace;"* (Ephesians 1:7).

Furthermore, when we ask God to forgive our sins, we must be willing to also forgive others. Forgiving others can be difficult when we don't follow the example demonstrated time after time when God forgives us. *"And be ye kind one to another, tenderhearted, forgiving one another, even as God for Christ's sake hath forgiven you"* (Ephesians 4:32). Unless we release our resentment and expectations of how we feel others' should respond with remorse, *we* will continue to give power to the situation and remain in bondage of their offense. *"[14]For if ye forgive men their trespasses [wrongful acts], your heavenly Father will also forgive you: [15]But if ye forgive not men their trespasses, neither will your Father forgive your trespasses"* (Matthew 6:14,15).

Her prayer acknowledged that through everything she faced, God has never given up on her. Whenever we feel like God has left us, we should be sure that we haven't left God. Sometimes when we choose to go our own way or handle things the way we see fit, we lose sight of the Lord and wonder why He seems so distant. He's not, He's right there waiting for us to return to Him. *"...for he hath said, I will never leave thee, nor forsake thee" (Hebrews 13:5b).*

Since God has never given up on us, we should never give up on God. We can endure the course of uncertainty because we understand that unfavorable times will happen and they are only a part of life while we are on Earth, as we look forward to eternal life with our Lord.

> [8]*We are troubled on every side, yet not distressed; we are perplexed, but not in despair; [9]Persecuted, but not forsaken; cast down, but not destroyed; [10]Always bearing about in the body the dying of the Lord Jesus, that the life also of Jesus might be made manifest in our body. [11]For we which live are alway[s] delivered unto death for Jesus' sake, that the*

life also of Jesus might be made manifest in our mortal flesh. ¹⁷For our light affliction, which is but for a moment, worketh for us a far more exceeding and eternal weight of glory;" (2 Corinthians 4:8-11,17).

"³⁷ . . . in all these things we are more than conquerors through him that loved us. ³⁸For I am persuaded, that neither death, nor life, nor angels, nor principalities, nor powers, nor things present, nor things to come, ³⁹Nor height, nor depth, nor any other creature, shall be able to separate us from the love of God, which is in Christ Jesus our Lord" (Romans 8:37-39).

As she continued to pray, she seemed to become stronger and spoke with assurance in the Lord. The more we communicate with God the more confident we become in His love for us, and no longer worry about our situation. God will provide. *"Behold the fowls of the air: for they sow not, neither do they reap, nor gather into barns; yet your heavenly Father feedeth them. Are ye not much better than they?"* (Matthew 6:26). In other words, just as the Lord provides for the birds, He will certainly provide for us.

She thanked God for loving her enough to sacrifice His only Son's life for her salvation. God demonstrated His love for us by sacrificing His only begotten Son, Jesus Christ. God's love surpasses all forms of love because He is love (1 John 4:8). *"For God so loved the world, that he gave his only begotten Son, that whosoever believeth in him should not perish, but have everlasting life"* (John 3:16).

Praying for guidance, she expressed her trust in God to bring her through her situation. The Lord has given us the Holy Spirit (the Comforter) who will guide us through every situation as we follow Christ. The Holy Spirit is always present, holding us up and keeping us from falling. Jesus said, *"¹⁶And I will pray the Father, and he shall give you another Comforter, that he may abide with you for ever;* (John 14:16).

While she prayed, she demonstrated faith in God as she turned all her cares over to Him—trusting and believing that He was right there with her and that He would answer her prayer. I was blessed to be present during her prayer while she freely expressed what was on her heart. As she reached out to the Lord, I prayed that God would use me as an instrument of encouragement (Romans 15:1, 2). Though she was new to the faith, she trusted God completely for her breakthrough.

Comments | God's Word in Prayer: Scriptures, Part 1

God's Word in Prayer: Scriptures, Part 2

PRAYER HELPS STRENGTHEN a believer's relationship with Christ. While referencing Scriptures that applied to my friend's prayer, I decided to include additional Scriptures that may help others grow closer to God through prayer.

When we pray, we must submit to God's will before we make our request, as Jesus did when He prayed in the Garden of Gethsemane (Luke 22:39-44).

Prayer conveys our trust in God, whether or not we understand or agree with His will. *"⁵Trust in the Lord with all thine heart; and lean not unto thine own understanding. ⁶In all your ways acknowledge him, and he shall direct thy paths"* (Proverbs 3:5-6).

We should not be anxious when we pray about a situation. Instead, give praise and thankfulness to God for what He has done and what He is about to manifest in our lives. The Apostle Paul reminds us that we must *"⁶Be careful for nothing [don't worry about* *anything]; but in everything by prayer and supplication with thanksgiving let your requests be made known unto God. ⁷And the peace of God, which passeth all understanding, shall keep your hearts and minds through Christ Jesus"* (Philippians 4:6-7).

Praying in the midst of others does not require an elaborate presentation. We are speaking to God not to the people around us. God is not impressed with empty, extravagant prayers intended to gain the approval of others. *"And when thou prayest, thou shalt not be as the hypocrites are [insincere]: for they love to pray standing in the synagogues and in the corners of the streets, that they may be seen of men. Verily [truly] I say unto, They have their reward"* (Matthew 6:5). God is pleased when we come to Him with sincerity and praise.

Jesus said, *". . . Be not afraid, only believe"* (Mark 5:36b). **If we struggle with believing and waiting on God in faith, then say what the father of an afflicted son said,** *". . . Lord, I believe; help thou mine [my] unbelief"* (Mark 9:24b).

Pray for strength for yourself and for others. The following is a prayer by the Apostle Paul in his letter to the Ephesians and to all who are faithful in Christ Jesus.

¹⁴For this cause I bow my knees unto the Father of our Lord Jesus Christ, ¹⁵Of whom the whole family in heaven and earth is named, ¹⁶That he would grant you, according to the riches of his glory, to be strengthened with might by his Spirit in the inner man; ¹⁷That Christ may dwell in your hearts by faith; that ye, being rooted and grounded in love, ¹⁸May be able to comprehend with all saints what is the breadth, and length, and depth, and height; ¹⁹And to know the love of Christ, which passeth knowledge, that ye might be filled with all the fulness of God. ²⁰Now unto him that is able to do exceeding abundantly above all that we ask or think, according to the power that worketh in us, ²¹Unto him be glory in the church by Christ Jesus throughout all ages, world without end. Amen." (Ephesians 3:14-21).

Pray in faith and with patience that God will open doors of opportunity. God is faithful and He will answer our prayers if we wait patiently for Him to reveal His plan.

> *"28Hast thou not known? Hast thou not heard, that the everlasting God, the Lord, the Creator of the ends of the earth, fainteth not, neither is weary? There is no searching of his understanding. 29He giveth power to the faint; and to them that have no might he increaseth strength. 30Even the youths shall faint and be weary, and the young men shall utterly fall: 31But they that wait upon the Lord shall renew their strength; they shall mount up with wings as eagles; they shall run, and not be weary; and they shall walk, and not faint."* (Isaiah 40:28-31).

Don't grow weary in doing all that we can to the glory of God; nor surrender to the uncertainties of our situations. Stay encouraged especially when the trials seem unbearable or as if they will never end. Keep praying and stay focused on what God is leading us to do so we won't be distracted by the deceptions of adversity. *"And let us not be weary in well-doing: for in due season we shall reap, if we faint not"* (Galatians 6:9).

Keep praying (1 Thessalonians 5:17), **believing in faith that God will answer our prayer;** *"Praying always with all prayer and supplication in the Spirit, and watching thereunto with all perseverance and supplication for all saints"* (Ephesians 6:18).

Make prayer a part of our daily regimen and watch God make a difference in our lives. *"Evening, and morning, and at noon, will I pray, and cry aloud: and he shall hear my voice"* (Psalm 55:17).

Comments | God's Word in Prayer: Scriptures, Part 2

A Spirit of Humility

THIS MORNING I woke up around 6:40 a.m. with pain in my lower back and neck. Basically, these symptoms were the results of a pickup truck slamming into the back of my car several years ago. Regardless of how I feel, I thank God for waking me and watching over me throughout the day.

As I continued getting ready for work, I started thinking about how my husband has worked two jobs for over six years—a full-time plus a part-time job three days a week. Working with the uncertainty of a volatile economy and also experiencing occasional back pain from a previous injury, he has shown tremendous love and commitment to help support our family. He stays focused on what God is leading him to do (Ephesians 6:6,7) and never worries about anyone else's opinion (Colossians 3:23)—*"Knowing that whatsoever good thing any man doeth, the same shall he receive of the Lord, . . ."* (Ephesians 6:8).

I am sure there are days when he doesn't feel like working the extra hours. Still, not once has he ever complained. I thank God for him and I continue praying that he will let go of the extra hours soon. For his spirit of humility and dedication, I am truly grateful.

God has given each of us abilities that are assets, allowing our family to function and stay encouraged. As we continue growing in our relationship with Christ, over the years, we have learned how to strengthen each other's weaknesses and benefit from each other's strengths (Proverbs 27:17). We have certainly had our share of obstacles, and we thank God for providing everything we need to keep moving forward with His plan for our lives. I believe that our strength is in having the right attitude about pleasing God in order to fulfill what God has called each of us to do.

I am very blessed to have a husband who loves God and keeps Him first in his life. This gives him inner strength, a sense of peace that he maintains through every situation no matter what comes our way. I am thankful that he trusts God to lead him as he leads our family. This doesn't mean that he does everything perfectly, but he is fully committed to the One who gives him perfect instructions. For that, I am sure that God is very pleased with his efforts and I am too.

Finally, my husband has been a light of encouragement for everyone he meets. Who knows, maybe his second job is not just for our family, but for him to also touch the lives of his coworkers and the customers that enter the store each day. With all things considered, my gratitude is not only for my husband, but most of all for my God who blessed me with him.

Comments | Spirit of Humility

TUESDAY, JANUARY 11, 7:25 P.M.

People, Read Your Bible!

WHEN REFERRING TO the Bible, some people may first recall the epic life of Jesus Christ, as well as the miraculous faith demonstrated by Moses, Noah, and Esther just to name a few. Being aware of such amazing individuals and their victories is very encouraging; but is awareness enough to continue growing as a believer in Christ?

Reading the Bible for ourselves in its entirety allows us to experience the most incredible journey of inspiration. When we read the Bible, the Holy Spirit teaches us (1 Corinthians 2:13) and brings to light the purpose and meaning of God's Word as we seek to learn more about Him. While exploring the depths of truth (1 Corinthians 2:10) and the foundation of life, we hear God's voice speaking to our spirit as He reveals His plan for our lives (1 Corinthians 2:12).

Over the years I have noticed that many faith-based studies primarily focus on the well-known Biblical characters and events that believers could readily relate to for Christian living. Though we are greatly encouraged by the faithfulness of Abraham, strengthened by the resilience of Joseph, and amazed by the miraculous parting of the Red Sea, the Bible contains a wealth of applicable principles for spiritual growth that we have yet to explore.

Every word of the Bible is true, written by the hands of appointed men inspired by God, and is essential for building a strong relationship with Christ. From time to time, I have met people who refer to the Bible as merely a book of ancient history or a fictional tale. Some choose to believe that the Bible is not worth reading because they think it is only about lessons of what we should and should not do—rewarding those who follow instructions and punishing those who do not. They are afraid that if they read the Bible, they will have to change their ways (Hebrews 4:12) and they would rather continue doing whatever they please.

Still others refer to the Bible as a book of stories about unlikely events that have nothing to do with present day. Contrary to this misconception, the Bible provides several references that reflect modern times, such as supporting our families (1 Timothy 5:8), feeding the hungry (Matthew 25:37), providing for the poor and homeless (Matthew 25:38), honoring and caring for veterans (John 15:13) and the elderly (Leviticus 19:32; Psalm 71:9), and preserving and protecting the environment (Genesis 2:15). It even references instances of individuals committing crimes motivated by lust (2 Samuel 11:1-18), instigating or gossiping (Ezra 4:6-24), publically judging other's sin and shame (John 8:1-11), and wrongfully accusing the innocent (John 18:1-12). However, the most important link between Biblical and modern times is Jesus Christ our Lord and Savior (Hebrews 13:8). His mission to save the lost will continue for generations to come.

Sin is becoming so common today that it seems to be expected. Currently, the world is more inclined to sin as technology and other vehicles of influences continue to progress. Though the Bible clearly defines sin, people of modern times wrongfully pick and choose what they want to believe.

There is always a choice between doing *what seems right by man* [an individual] (Proverbs 14:12; 16:25) and doing *what is right by God* (Psalm 1:1-4; 37:4). Yet, in this day and time, some people question God's Word, especially concerning issues that affect their personal preferences. Certainly some of the practices and prohibitions in Biblical history do not apply to our way of life today. However, that which is *against God* (Psalm 51:4) is sin. Those who disagree try to justify their opinion based on the truth that *we are no longer under the law, we are under grace* (Romans 6:14). However, this Scripture tells us that through Jesus Christ, we are free from the *condemnation of sin* (Romans 8:1)—the shame, blame, and most of all eternal *death* (Romans 6:23). Jesus Christ alone paid the price for all our sins. Thus when we accept Him as our Lord and Savior, we have freedom from the *penalty* of sin, not freedom to sin. Many people tend to generalize the freedom Christ bought for us, and they try to use it to accommodate their personal preferences that are displeasing to God.

Profanity, for instance, though disrespectful to God and to others, is fairly common to hear. It is one of many unrighteous acts against God (Romans 3:9-14) that many of us are either guilty of speaking or guilty of allowing it to be spoken in our presence without speaking against it in the name of the Lord. The blasphemous use of God and Jesus Christ (Leviticus 18:21b) has slipped into everyday conversations as just another form of expression. It is unproductive and destructive.

Some people may use these words out of fear or denial (Matthew 26:74), for humor to get attention or approval, or out of anger to reflect a message of power. Instead, the real message they send is of weakness and disrespect for themselves, others, and most of all God. Proverbs 15:4 tells us that *"a wholesome tongue is a tree of life: but perverseness therein is a breach in the spirit."*

Psalm 19:14 says, *"Let the words of my mouth, and the meditation of my heart, be acceptable in thy sight, O Lord, my strength, and my redeemer."* As we refrain from using words that are displeasing to God we set an example for others and become more effective for Christ. This allows us to reach the heart of the lost to help them overcome their stronghold(s). By reading the Bible consistently, we plant God's Word in our hearts so the Holy Spirit will help us understand and apply what we have studied. Then we are able to share the love of Christ more effectively with others.

As with profanity, homosexuality is also becoming more common in our culture today, even though the Bible clearly states in Leviticus 18:22 that God calls this immoral behavior abomination [sin]. Some people today do not consider homosexuality a sin because it was condemned in the Old Testament, even though it is also condemned in the New Testament (Romans 1:26,27; 1 Timothy 1:8-11). They try to justify their opinion with Romans 6:14 because we are no longer under the law that was given by God in the Old Testament days. However, to my understanding, what this Scripture actually conveys is that because of God's grace we are free from having to pay the price of sin through death, since Jesus already paid for all our sins with His life. This Scripture does not mean that we are free to continue in sin.

Advocates of homosexuality try to compare it to other Biblically historical practices that no longer apply to our lifetime. However, these practices were not defined by God as an abomination (sin). Those who are familiar with Scripture may mention how the Lord (in Leviticus Chapter 11) refers to eating certain foods as an abomination (unfit), mainly meat from animals that chew their cud or have divided hoofs. Yet, they forget to mention how, through the Spirit, the Lord clarified what makes foods acceptable that would otherwise be unfit (1 Timothy 4:3-5). He said as long as food is received with thanksgiving, sanctified[4] by the Word of God and prayer, it is acceptable. Nowhere in the Bible, to my understanding, does God change His mind about homosexuality.

The Apostle Paul addresses the consequences of this lifestyle and other immoral behaviors in 1 Corinthians 6:9,10. Though I believe the consequence that Paul mentioned about *not being able to inherit the kingdom of God,* applies to those who choose to remain in sin without any desire to repent and turn to the Lord. Essentially, anyone remaining in a life of homosexuality ignores what God intended when He created woman to be the only suitable partner for man.

"18And the Lord God said, It is not good that the man should be alone; I will make him an help meet [one suitable] for

him. [19]And out of the ground the Lord God formed every beast of the field, and every fowl of the air; and brought them unto Adam to see what he would call them: and whatsoever Adam called every living creature, that was the name thereof. [20]And Adam gave names to all cattle, and to the fowl of the air, and to every beast of the field; but for Adam there was not found an help meet [one suitable] for him. [21]And the Lord God caused a deep sleep to fall upon Adam, and he slept: and he took one of his ribs, and closed up the flesh instead thereof; [22]And the rib, which the Lord God had taken from man, made he a woman, and brought her unto the man" (Genesis 2:18-22). Thus, God created a woman for a man, not a man for a man or a woman for a woman.

Surely there were certain practices of Biblical times that no longer apply today: stoning the accused, sacrificing animals for the atonement of sin, permitting slavery, and limiting the role of women in ministry. Still, God did not call these practices sin. As for homosexuality, God specifically called it an abomination *(translated in the Bible as sin)*. Basically, those who are committed to a life of homosexuality have been deceived by the enemy (Satan) as an attempt to destroy the fulfillment of God's Creation. Some individuals justify this lifestyle by believing that God allows them to live this way because they are born this way. Based on the Word of God, I believe they are born this way because we are all born in sin. Psalm 51:5 says *"Behold, I was shapen in iniquity, and in sin did my mother conceive me."* This is true because of the original sin that was committed by Adam when he and Eve were deceived by Satan. Prior to salvation, we all share the "consequence of the first sin" (eternal death). Though we are born in sin, with the help of the Holy Spirit, we can walk away from sin when we turn our lives over to Christ and receive salvation by the grace of God (Ephesians 2:8). Jesus said, *"I am the way, the truth, and the life: no man cometh unto the father, but by me"* (John 14:6).

Profanity and homosexuality are just two examples of how sin is becoming more common today. But as we read the Bible regularly and apply God's Word, we will find encouragement to overcome sin that tries to distract us from the promises of God. Though becoming more widespread, sin has plagued humanity for years. The Bible teaches that there is nothing new. Everything stems from an original existence—God's Creation. *"The thing that hath been, it is that which shall be; and that which is done is that which shall be done: and there is no new thing under the sun"* (Ecclesiastes 1:9).

When we read the Bible regularly, we can learn from the choices and even the mistakes individuals made in those days because the Bible depicts real situations similar to what we go through today. These situations are encountered by people who have some of the same desires and expectations for their lives that we have for our lives. How they deal with their situations depends on in whom or what they place their faith. Basically, there are two types of individuals. Those who reverence God and those who reject Him. Overall, the Bible gives an interesting account of what happens in both cases.

Though God is in complete control, sometimes our choices contribute to the reason for certain unlikely events that occur in our lives. Other times they occur for the fulfillment of God's plan, *". . . that the works of God should be made manifest [evident] in him"* (John 9:3b). For instance, the Bible contains stories about certain individuals God allowed to act in ways that may otherwise be considered questionable from the human perspective (e.g., an unlawful act (Daniel Chapter 6), an intentional social visit with sinners (Mark 2:13-17), and the death of an innocent man (Luke Chapter 23)). The purpose is that these situations were necessary for the fulfillment of God's plan.

Reading the Bible for ourselves in its entirety allows us to see how the world looks from God's perspective. When we study the Bible, we begin to understand why we stumble following our will, and why we are blessed following God's. As we open our Bibles, we stand at the threshold of hope where we can choose to step into the light or remain in darkness.

The Bible is life's key that we hold in our hands, though it can only access the blessings of God if we use it regularly. The Bible is the description of life before, during, and after Christ Jesus. It explains why we do what we do and feel as we feel. It provides the applicable principles that teach us how to survive the unexpected and live victoriously through Christ.

As Christians, our natural tendency is to do whatever we desire, and anything that doesn't fit comfortably into our agenda we disregard. But if we want to live victoriously through Christ, reading the Bible is the best place to start. Finding the time to read the Bible seems to be the biggest issue. For instance, if you don't have time to read before you go to work in the morning, try reading during one of your breaks. Pray before you start reading, and ask for wisdom and understanding so you can apply the principles of God's Word effectively. Pray also, that He will allow you to be a light to others.

There is no excuse not to read the Bible, with ample resources available through ministry websites such as Family of Faith Ministries™ (FoFM™) at *www.fofm.us*. When you selectively research ministry resources on the Internet, you can download Biblical content to your computer, cell phone, and tablet PC. These and other electronic or mobile devices can provide convenient access to God's Word anytime and anywhere. Soon, new advances in technology will produce even greater opportunities to study God's Word. So read the Bible and start effectively living the Living Word of God while He is still near (Isaiah 55:6).

Comments | People, Read Your Bible!

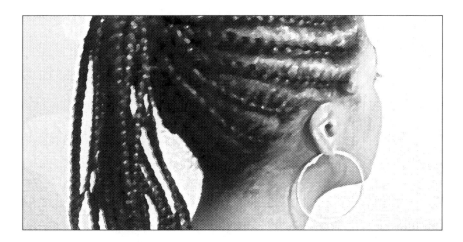

Sisters

RELATIONSHIPS ARE ONE of God's Creations that develop over time. Initially they are perceived as a natural occurrence, but they are actually part of God's Master Plan, designed with a purpose. *"To every thing there is a season, and a time to every purpose under the heaven:"* (Ecclesiastes 3:1). A relationship with Jesus Christ is established primarily for the purpose of salvation. Though a very important part of God's plan, this relationship occurs by the choice God gives each of us to accept or reject His Son Jesus Christ. However, the relationships we have with our families by birth are not by choice. We are born into the families God intended, though we have the choice to either nurture or neglect family relationships.

One of the most unique family relationships God created is between sisters. Though sisters may not always get along, unity will remain for those who embrace the spiritual bond that connects them as a family. I am focusing on this particular relationship because I come from a family of six girls—which I see as a very unique blessing from God. I believe it is in God's plan that some mothers give birth to all girls, creating a unit of similar individuals with a common bond, yet different with specific purposes. While it is crucial for each sister to form her own identity as an individual, it is just as important for each to interact with each other for the purpose of the relationship God created. This purpose may be to develop a strong support system so that each sister will function more effectively as individuals.

During this semester of my graduate studies, I had to work on an assignment about groups and teams. Groups are a more informal gathering of individuals that casually come together with a "common interest." Teams come together for a "specific purpose." The research for this assignment led me to realize that one of the most important teams of which I am a member is the team of *sisters*—purposefully created by God.

As I continued thinking about this realization, I noticed that in the center of the word SISTERS is the letter "T," which I associated with the word "team." The three letters on each side of the letter "T" reminds me of how the six of us make up a set of three older and three younger sisters. Together as a team we are six strong, talented, beautifully created women *". . . fearfully and wonderfully made . . ."* by God (Psalm 139:14). Our goal as a team is to serve as a support system for each other—working together as a unique creation of God. This team will thrive as long as its members are actively building a strong and viable relationship, communicating and creating a common bond that will further develop each member individually. In other words, this team allows each member to also pursue her individual purpose so that the team collectively glorifies God.

Love is a very important ingredient in any relationship. Without love, relationships struggle to serve the purpose for which God has planned. According to 1 Corinthians 13, love is *not selfish, not easily provoked, or offended.* Therefore love is crucial to maintain a viable relationship between sisters no matter what situations may arise. Though sisters sometimes have differences, there will always be a bond that will never be broken because no one can divide what is united by God (Mark 10:9).

Spiritually, the team of sisters will always be united, regardless of geographic location, age, or personality.

Sisters by birth are not given the opportunity to choose who will be on their team. God specifically selects each individual to fulfill His overall plan. It is up to each member to work together to successfully operate as a viable unit, interacting with each other, encouraging and strengthening each other to ultimately make an impact for Christ.

Though communication is essential, sisters do not have to call each other every day. However, they should make an honest effort to support each other by communicating regularly in the good times and the trying times. In doing so, their bond is strengthened rather than merely existent with only a few calls or visits on special occasions. Their bond is also strengthened by the respect they have for each other—accepting each other's differences and appreciating the value that each brings to the team. This level of respect is evident in the genuine love and concern each sister demonstrates towards each other.

A sister team is victorious as long as love and respect continues while there is still time. Otherwise, soon enough, team members will finish their season and have to go home. Time is very precious in any relationship.

All things considered, sisters are a team with a God-given purpose that they should not take lightly or for granted. If you have a sister, stay in touch. Don't let anyone or anything isolate you from God's incredible creation. The success of each sister is even greater for those who cherish and actively participate in their *sister team* because each individual on the team needs each other to fulfill God's overall plan.

Comments | Sisters

Saved for a Purpose

LAST NIGHT I dreamed I was walking along a beach scattered with mounds of sand and dark sunken areas. I saw cave-like structures and people I didn't know. We were wandering around, but apparently for a reason. I walked further and noticed that the people looked as if they needed help but didn't know who to ask. Basically, it seemed as though we were all out there searching for something. We really didn't know what we were searching for, but we felt the urge to keep searching while everyone continued going his or her own way (Isaiah 53:6).

All of a sudden, as I took another step, I started sliding into one of the sunken areas that I didn't see in front of me. I tried to regain control but started sliding even faster. I raised my arms and shouted for help (Psalm 34:17;142:5-7; Romans 10:13), but everyone around me kept going their own way as if all they cared about was moving along the sand for as long as they could (Psalm 142:4).

Finally, I stopped sliding and was gently lifted out of my fall (Psalm 40:1,2). Though I did not feel a physical touch of anyone pulling me out, what I had fallen into was finally moving further and further away from me (Isaiah 41:9,10). This amazing rescue, this divine restoration, gave me peace, opened my eyes, and allowed me to *"... see, and know, and consider, and understand together, that the hand of the Lord hath done this, . . ."* (Isaiah 41:20). I was saved, lifted *". . . out of darkness into his marvellous light:"* (1 Peter 2:9).

Once again I was walking along the beach. But this time, since I was saved, my life had new meaning. I was no longer aimlessly wandering and falling into the darkness of uncertainty. Instead, I was living a life of purpose—a life that reflects the Light of Christ to share with others (Matthew 28:19,20; Mark 16:15,16; Luke 24:46-48).

Comments | Saved for a Purpose

God's Love Is Forever

"THERE'S NOTHING YOU can do to make God stop loving you because there's nothing you did to make Him start." Hearing these words from a Christian radio host one morning on my way to work was the perfect reminder that God's love is forever (Jeremiah 31:3). He loves us so deeply (Isaiah 43:3,4) not because there's anything special that we could ever do for Him. He loves us because we are His creation, an original plan He wrote well before our time (Jeremiah 1:5). Not only did God create us, but He made sure that we have the provisions to fulfill our unique purpose. He carefully planned every detail so that nothing is left to what some people believe as luck or chance. Why? Because God has been and will always be in complete control.

No matter what you've done in the past, once you have accepted the Son of God (Jesus Christ) as your Lord and Savior, you will experience the love of God forever. But if you choose to reject Christ and continue living an unsaved[7] life, you are not covered by the blood of Jesus through His sacrifice on the cross (Luke 19:10; 1 Corinthians 15:1-4). Instead, you are living life on your own—depending on your limited efforts, abilities, and provisions, which belong to God. When you reject God you disregard His will for your life and ultimately forfeit the blessings He has planned for you. These are the blessings that only God can provide that will last forever. Perhaps following your own way may make you successful by the world's definition; however, at some point you may realize that it's not enough.

Though God unconditionally loves and forgives, His grace doesn't give us the freedom to purposefully disregard the life that He has planned for us. Instead, He wants us to turn from our sins (Ephesians 4:22-25), do what is right (Deuteronomy 6:18) for His glory. He knows that we will fall short at times and because of His love, forgiveness, mercy, and grace, if we honestly admit and turn away from our wrongdoings (1 John 1:9), God welcomes us back into a right relationship with Him through Christ Jesus. God will always be with us no matter what (Joshua 1:5; Hebrews 13:5), but when our lives do not reflect His love we may have to face the consequences of our actions to help us grow and make better decisions. Even still, God is right there with us (Psalm 23:4).

Following God's will is only as possible as Christians are willing to make God's will their first priority—as did Christ (Luke 2:49). The more we come to know Christ through reading the Bible and being receptive of the Holy Spirit, the more we learn and grow from life's experiences. Then we will be able to hear His voice and follow His call (John 10:27-30). When we follow Christ we choose to walk in the Spirit and not in the flesh. Walking in the Spirit of God allows us to deny the worldly desires of the flesh that are triggered by human emotions and distractions. *"11For the grace of God that bringeth salvation hath appeared to all men. 12Teaching us that, denying ungodliness and worldly lusts, we shall live soberly, righteously, and godly, in this present world;"* (Titus 2:11-12).

As followers of Christ, we seek to lay aside all deceitful selfish desires, and take on a brand new life created in the likeness of God (2 Corinthians 5:15, 17). One would think that once we have chosen to follow Christ we would be committed to Him because He is the Son of God, the Almighty King of Heaven and Earth. But because we do not see God with our physical sight, we tend to slip into spiritual amnesia—forgetting what God has already done, and focusing on the temptations that distract and lead us to sin. Therefore, as long as we live in the flesh, we have to deny the cravings of our sinful nature *daily* in order to follow the will of God (Matthew 16:24).

The Apostle Paul wrote in Romans 7:14-25 of how he would die to his flesh (deny temptations) daily. In other words, he had to continually look to God to keep from giving into his human nature. Temptations that come between God and man could be as explicit as the desire to steal something out of greed, spite, or perceived necessity. They are also as implicit as not forgiving others or denying your faith in public.

Whether or not you are a believer in Christ, as long as you are in this world, you will face moments of temptation (Matthew 26:41). This is why Christians must always rely on the Holy Spirit to stay right with God and represent Christ well. It is difficult for the unsaved[7] to see how much they really need Christ when they see Christians struggling to follow Him. When we claim to love God but constantly fall to temptations, or worry and fall apart during the tough times of life, the unsaved[7] feel they might as well live their own way because our response to adversity is no different than how they would respond. God never promised that life would be easy or meet our expectations. Instead, He promised to love and protect us, though He will not spoil us or prevent things from happening that would otherwise teach, humble, and even restore us. Still, no matter what, God is always present to help us work through every situation and circumstance we face (Psalm 46:1). God is fully aware of the detours we sometimes choose to take, so He prepared a Way for us to return to Him through His Son Jesus Christ. He is the only Way (John 14:6) that we can remain committed to God and respond to the guidance of the Holy Spirit.

Those who accept Christ as their Lord and Savior are adopted into the family of God and are no longer a slave to sin (Romans 6:16-18). The consequence of not accepting Christ as your Lord and Savior yields eternal separation from God, which is far worse (Isaiah 26:20-21) than any unfavorable situation you will ever encounter in this life. But when you allow Christ to be Lord of your life, you experience the love of God that will last forever. *"Neither yield ye your members [any part of yourself] as instruments of unrighteousness unto sin: but yield yourselves unto God, as those that are alive from the dead, and your members as instruments of righteousness unto God"* (Romans 6:13).

Comments | God's Love is Forever

Two Birds

GOD PLACES PEOPLE in our lives at the right time and for the right reason to help mature us according to His will (Roman 15:1). There are those who sharpen our dull spirit, lift our low moments, and absolutely understand that we are all a work in progress. This connection creates a bond for life that affirms our existence and makes us complete. Though we have the support of others, we can only follow our path of life when we spread our wings and start flying.

Like birds we naturally desire to soar high above our current circumstances, to excel or advance in every aspect of our lives, including health, finances, family, friends, careers, possessions, and even our abilities. We envision reaching new heights to achieve our greatest expectations. Yet, only those who accept the challenge will reap the benefits of their faith. Figuratively speaking, there are essentially two types of birds: doubters who are too afraid to leave the nest, and believers who are ready to fly.

The doubters will question any inkling of change and may choose to stay safe in the nest. As a result, they may forego the experiences that are necessary to realize their purpose. They dream dreams and see visions of their future but they lack the faith that will help them make it happen.

After some time, they begin to view their dreams as farfetched or impossible because their outlook is faded by unpleasant memories or experiences yoked with the fear of failure. They see life from their current perspective and convince themselves to accept that this is the best they can do or else God would have allowed them to do better by now.

Doubters may be miserable in their current situation, but they seldom try to change it for improvement. Others who truly care about them may try to make suggestions, but doubters immediately cling to what they already know and hide behind excuses as to why they can't change their course or why they believe their supporters' suggestions won't work. Their resistance actually exhausts their time and energy to get up and fly. Then finally, they come to the conclusion that their current situation has become their norm and any changes at this point would be impossible to achieve.

On the other hand, the believers not only seeks change but they embrace it because they have a strong desire to rise even higher than their current situation if it is God's will. They are faithful in that they don't move without God, but rather they watch, and are ready for His next instruction because they know that God is always with them (Isaiah 41:10). They listen with the discernment[1] of the Holy Spirit, and are able to draw from others' spirit-based input that may be essential to their journey. For the most part, believers gratefully utilize their God-given abilities and resources in order to achieve His perfect plan. All things considered, they allow the winds of their experiences to take them higher with each new flight.

Reaching for something new can be uneasy and yet exciting at the same time. There are no guarantees in life so we cannot say that everything we hope to achieve will come to past. Besides, God did not promise to fulfill "our" hopes and dreams. He promised that His perfect will ". . . *will be done in earth, as it is in heaven*" (Matthew 6:10). Believers respond to God's call. They are ready and willing to spread their wings and soar across new territory. Which of the two birds are you?

Comments | Two Birds

SPRING SECTION

What's in a Moment?

A MOMENT IS gone at the start of another and all that matters is what will happen next. At least that's what we think about when we are ready to move beyond our current situation. Though we can't help but wonder when our most trying times will turn around, they only last as long as God allows them to fulfill their purpose for our spiritual growth (Genesis 50:20).

We remain encouraged and continue seeking God for direction by *casting all our cares on Him because He cares for us* (1 Peter 5:7). By letting go of the reins of life, the Lord will guide us in the right direction as we learn to trust Him even more. But for some of us, depending on God is easier said than done because we still end up trying to control our own lives. We try to rush through the moments of life that are contrary to our plans when we can't see how God is using them for our good. Since God's response to our situation is not always obvious, we start doing what we think will work, which generally causes a setback. Then, when we finally get out of God's way, as soon as He solves one problem we are ready to complain or worry about the next before we realize what we should have learned from the first. All we are concerned with is the situation at hand, and when will it get better. It's a natural human reaction because certainly no one wants to go through the unfavorable. We just have to keep learning to look beyond every situation as if it is already resolved, because in God's time, it is.

Though we never know what will happen next, we should always be ready and willing to see our situations from God's perspective, and trust that God will see us through in His perfect time. *"¹⁷For our light affliction, which is but for a moment, worketh for us a far more exceeding and eternal weight of glory; ¹⁸While we look not at the things which are seen, but at the things which are not seen: for the things which are seen are temporal; but the things which are not seen are eternal"* (2 Corinthians 4:17,18). Every moment of life is precious because each contains an essential portion of God's plan for our lives.

Comments | What's in a Moment?

SATURDAY, MARCH 12, 8:30 A.M.

About Tithing

JUST AS THERE are many views and concerns about any subject pertaining to money, tithing is no exception. Tithing is a form of giving. It is a part of worship and acknowledgement of the Lord we serve. It is one of the commandments God gave to Moses for the children of Israel at the foot of Mount Sinai (Leviticus 27:34) and is essentially one tenth of our increase (Numbers 18:21).

The Controversy (Tithe or not tithe?) Many believers have stopped tithing because of their interpretation of the Scripture, *"For Christ is the end of the law for righteousness to every one that believeth"* (Romans 10:4). Thus, they believe that the law is cancelled and no longer necessary to follow. They believe that we should no longer tithe, as the law is already fulfilled by Christ. However, the purpose of tithing, even today, is not to fulfill the law; but rather, to demonstrate our love for God. Surely there are other ways to demonstrate our love, but through God's Word we know that tithing is what He requested of His people (Leviticus 27:30). Just as we eagerly look to give others what they request, we can certainly do the same for our Lord.

Furthermore, the law was not solely about tithing. Therefore, if we choose to stop tithing, then why not claim the right to stop following other commands of God that shape our moral standards today? God's principles remain because God never changes (Malachi 3:6; Hebrews 13:8). Instead, we try to change His principles to fit our expectations and plans, and cover our doubts and fears. Many who argue against tithing, focus on how giving tithes depletes their personal finances substantially, rather than positions them to prosper. These individuals keep forgetting about the blessings God provides every day. They are actually telling God that they do not trust Him with the finances that they give through the church in support of the ministry. Their main concern is how much they are giving up, rather than how their givings are an expression of Who they love more than anything (Luke 10:27).

God's love for us is evident in the blessings we take for granted every day, and He helps us stay focused through the written guidance He already provided for our living. The law was given so we would clearly understand what is considered sin, *". . . for by the law is the knowledge of sin"* (Romans 3:20). *"What shall we say then? Is the law sin? God forbid. Nay, I had not known sin, but by the law . . ."* (Romans 7:7). Thus, God gave the law so that we will know the difference between right and wrong.

Sin is the transgression of the law (1 John 3:4), and with sin there are consequences. *"For the wages of sin is death"* (Romans 6:23a), though no longer a physical death, yet far worst—spiritual death and separation from God. *"But the gift of God is eternal life through Jesus Christ our Lord"* (Romans 6:23b), for Christ was manifested (revealed) to destroy the works of the devil (1 John 3:8b). When Christ, in Whom there was no sin (1 John 3:5b), gave His life for us, we were made free from the bondage of sin (Galatians 5:1) so that we may have eternal life. Only through Christ Jesus we are saved (John 14:6). Thus, following God's commandments provides guidance for living effectively through Christ as a result of salvation, not to earn salvation. *"2For the law of the Spirit of life in Christ Jesus hath made me free from the law of sin and death. 4That the righteousness [ordinance] of the law might be fulfilled in us, who walk not after the flesh, but after the Spirit"* (Romans 8:2,4).

The law allows us to live orderly with one another and keep God first through our tithes. Prioritizing God is about placing Him before all else, especially what we value most. In many cases, money is at the top of our list of most valuable earthly possessions. We may think it is our family, but our focus is revealed when we place our jobs over participating in their lives, for instance. As a reflection of our tendencies regarding money, our finances parallel our level of trust. When we faithfully tithe we express our trust in God, that He is valued more than everything, even the most sought-after possession on Earth. Otherwise, how then can we say we trust God and yet we ignore or try to compromise any part of His instruction—tithing? We cannot pick and choose what portion of God's Word we will believe or follow. For example, when we accept salvation, we willingly respond to all that we must do to be saved[5] (John 3:5-7; Romans 10:9,10). As part of the text of the entire Bible, tithing must not be ignored, for *"[16]All scripture is given by inspiration of God, and is profitable for doctrine, for reproof, for correction, for instruction in righteousness: [17]That the man of God may be perfect, throughly furnished unto all good works* (2 Timothy 3:16,17). *"Wherefore the law is holy, and the commandment holy, and just, and good"* (Romans 7:12).

In Matthew 5:17 the Lord says, *"Think not that I am come to destroy the law, or the prophets: I am not come to destroy, but to fulfil."* The fulfillment of the law means that His death, burial, and resurrection fulfilled the initial purpose of the law (Luke 19:10; 1 Corinthians 15:1-4). We are made right with God through Christ Jesus and therefore are saved by the grace of God, not by anything that we can do or else we would claim that the victory of deliverance is due to our own efforts (Ephesians 2:8,9).

Through the new covenant, Christ placed the laws upon our hearts and wrote them in our minds (Hebrews 10:16) so we will always know right from wrong. Though we will be judged, not at the expense of salvation, but held accountable by God for our actions on Earth. The Apostle Paul said in Romans 2:16 that in the Day of Judgment God will *". . . judge the secrets of men by Jesus Christ"* according to His Gospel. Therefore we still need to be obedient in reverence to God.

All the law and the prophets are summed up by two main laws known as The Great Commandment which says, *"[37] . . . Thou shalt love the Lord thy God with all thy heart, and with all thy soul, and with all thy mind. [38] This is the first and great commandment. [39] And the second is like unto it, Thou shalt love thy neighbor as thyself"* (Matthew 22:37-39). These two laws are based on the principle of "love." *"Love worketh no ill to his neighbor: therefore love is the fulfilling of the law"* (Romans 13:10). The old laws that were given are now fulfilled by our love. When we *"bear ye one another's burdens, we fulfill [follow] the law of Christ"* (Galatians 6:2). Because the Lord is an advocate of order (1 Corinthians 14:40), He provides direction even into the last days, *". . . for the law shall go forth of Zion, and the word of the Lord from Jerusalem"* (Micah 4:1-2).

The law gives instruction and keeps order. So when we start getting away from God's instruction, we fall away from the purpose God has called us to fulfill. Because there are churches today that have lost their focus, some believers no longer give tithes to the church. These churches are more concerned with increasing givings, membership, and recognition, rather than developing disciples (learners) to further the kingdom. They are starting to look and operate more and more like the world, leaving a terrible impression for the young in faith and the skeptical.

As a result, many people have chosen to no longer come to the church to worship and study God's Word. Instead they rely solely on their independent Bible study, Christian books, Internet, or television ministries. Who can blame them when there are churches that resemble a social club or place to network a business rather than serve as the house of God? Having no *"storehouse"* to bring their tithes to the Lord (Malachi 3:10) these believers have decided not to tithe at all. They may believe in supporting the church financially and helping others in need, but they disagree with the way some churches try to manipulate parishioners into giving. Still, we should not disregard tithing based on whether or not a church meets our standards.

The church is responsible for teaching the principles of tithing. Yet, some churches seem to focus on emphasizing the consequences of not giving tithes (Malachi 3:8,9). It is necessary for churches to teach believers to give, but the approach is crucial for developing a committed body of believers. When churches are more concerned about *"receiving the tithes"* over *"teaching the principles of tithing,"* their efforts only reflect a lack of faith that God will supply the needs of the church. Then how can they set an example for the believers?

Considering the fact that some believers no longer tithe, churches must take care to make sure they provide a clear understanding of tithes so believers will realize God's blessing and not feel caught up in the church's agenda. When tithing appears to be solely supporting the mission of a church, believers start to lose sight of how tithing is also part of their worship to God. As a result, they begin to redirect their givings to what will support their personal efforts, forgetting that God provides everything they need. God warns us about pride when He mentioned how we refuse to keep His ordinances. He said, *"14Ye have said, . . . what profit is it that we have kept his ordinance . . . 15And now we call the proud happy . . ."* (Malachi 3:14;15).

What Right Do We Have to Question Tithing? While searching the Scriptures to learn about tithes, I could not find any Scriptures that specifically said *we should no longer bring our tithes* to the storehouse (the church) where the Lord told us to bring them in Malachi 3:10. God loves when *we give cheerfully what we purpose in our heart* (2 Corinthians 9:7). Likewise, we show love for Him when we tithe, as the principle of tithing reflects our attitude towards God. In Leviticus 27:10,13 we are reminded that when we dedicate a certain portion to the Lord we should keep our promise and not change the amount when it suddenly becomes a financial challenge. If we choose to commit our tithes to God, we should not withhold it when times are uncertain by misinterpreting the Scriptures to justify our position. We must be sure that what we choose to believe about giving is what God truly intended.

When you tithe your *increase* (your income and other financial blessings), set this portion aside first, *above all other spending*, to give back to God. He will honor your faithfulness. Among other ways that you give back to the Lord, including time, talents, and nonmonetary items, a financial blessing (money) is a practical way to support multiple areas of ministry (e.g., to help sustain the church and further outreach). Also when you tithe, pray that God will direct the church leaders to use the tithe for the *edification* (improvement) of the *body of Christ* (believers in Christ). Then pray over the remainder of your increase for direction in handling your finances wisely. Consider the remainder as if it is all that you have and then watch what God can do to sustain you and your family. Husbands and wives, and even income earning sons and daughters, may each tithe from their own increase. Tithing should be taken seriously to honor God because tithes are holy unto the Lord (Leviticus 27:30).

Tithing is a personal exercise of faith in a personal relationship with Christ (Hebrews 10:23). It is not a matter of giving our hard earned cash to a church or preacher who doesn't deserve it, or worrying over how the money is used by the church, but rather an act of obedience in faith to God. It is unfortunate that some believers start questioning whether or not to tithe when they have become disheartened with the way their church handles tithing. They feel pressured rather than instructed to follow this part of God's plan. They search the Scriptures to justify why they choose not to give, but many times their claim is based on their perspective of the church. All I can say is that we must always allow the Holy Spirit to guide us to the true interpretation of the Scriptures (John 16:13; 2 Timothy 2:15; 2 Timothy 3:16).

It is ironic how the self-righteous Sadducees and Pharisees (ancient Jewish aristocratic sects distinguished by strict interpretation of the traditional and written law) thought they knew what to expect at the coming of the Messiah. Yet they missed Him all together. He was right there, but they were so determined that Jesus was not the real deal, they rejected Him. To avoid such a crucial mistake, we should not withhold anything from God, particularly tithes, at the risk of misinterpretation or selfish pride.

In general, my thoughts about tithing are the results of praying for guidance and understanding as I searched the Scriptures. But I recommend others to search the Scriptures for themselves. *"Wisdom is the principal thing; therefore get wisdom: and with all thy getting get understanding"* (Proverbs 4:7). The following is a compilation of scriptural references in a general outline regarding tithes.

Beginning of Tithes. The first tithe was given by Abraham (Abram) who God blessed as the first great Biblical patriarch. Genesis Chapter 14 records the time when Abraham returned with his servants after defeating Chedorlaomer, king of Elam. When he was blessed by Melchizedek (King of Salem) for a victorious battle, Abraham gave him *"tithes of all"* (Genesis 14:20). You can also find a reference to Abraham tithing in Hebrews 7:2-4, which refers to Melchizedek (Melchisedec) as King of peace. Melchizedek was referred to as a *priest of the Most High God* in verse one. Giving tithes to Melchizedek reflects the importance of giving tithes to God.

Numbers 18:20-32 explains how the tithes offered by the children of Israel (descendants of Jacob) are given as *"an heave offering unto the Lord."* The heave offering was to be set apart, taken from the best (Exodus 29:27) as an inheritance for the Levites (one of the 12 tribes of Israel). God commanded the sons of Levi (chosen for the office of priesthood) to take (collect) tithes according to the law (Hebrews 7:5). As the Israelites gave tithes to God through the priesthood, we give tithes to God through the church.

Purpose of Tithes. *"Thou shalt truly tithe all the increase of thy seed, that the field bringeth forth year by year"* (Deuteronomy 14:22). The tithe must be set aside first before all else. By tithing we are expressing to God our desire to put Him first. We value the most what we do with our money first. Nehemiah 10:35 and Deuteronomy 18:4 reference the requirement of first fruits. Tithing allows us to focus our attention on God and reminds us that everything we have belongs to God (Colossians 1:15-17). In other words, we tithe what is of greatest personal value, to indicate that we value God the most.

The Israelites tithed a portion of their increase in agriculture and livestock which was of great value in Biblical times. Today we tithe a portion of the money we receive from our increase (income). Because the church provides a place of worship conducive to today's environmental conditions, running water, electricity, heating, and cooling are all standard requirements for the physical structure of the church. All of which require money, not food, to maintain the church facility. What we tithe today is appropriate for what the church requires to continue functioning as a light in the community. Today, when we honor God with our tithes, we are blessed by the benefits of supporting church ministry as well as the increase that God continues to provide through our occupations (Luke 6:38). Most of all, we are blessed to consume the riches of God's Spoken Word. Then we can live more effectively and share the Gospel of Jesus Christ so that others will come to know Him as their Lord and Savior.

Another purpose of tithing is to make provisions for those who are in need. The Lord instructed the Israelites in Deuteronomy 14:22 to bring the tithe annually. They were to *eat before the Lord, the tithes that they bring to the place where He chooses to place His name, so they will learn to fear [reverence] the Lord God always* (Deuteronomy 14:23). Items such as corn, wine, oil, and the firstborn of their herds and flocks are listed in the Scripture. Then every three years they were to bring the tithe as an inheritance for the Levites, and others at the gate so those who are in need will also be satisfied (Deuteronomy 14:27-29). These individuals were the Levite, the stranger, the fatherless, and the widow. The Levites did not inherit any portion of the land of Canaan (Joshua 14:3; Numbers 18:23; Deuteronomy 18:1-5) because they were called to serve in the tabernacle of the congregation. But they were given the tithe which is one tenth of the increase of the Israelites (Numbers 18:21,24) for their inheritance.

Food for Thought. Today, should we tithe livestock and food annually to eat at the place where we worship God? Also, should we give tithes every three years to support the pastors and the disadvantaged? We have to consider the differences of the culture and the customs of the people in Biblical times while we focus on the principle of tithing.

What's significant in the instructions is that they were to tithe the first of their increase. As far as how often, raising livestock and reaping the harvest from crops takes longer than reaping the benefits from the income that we receive today through non-agricultural occupations. Whether we bring our tithe annually, monthly, biweekly, or weekly based on the pay period of our place of employment, the importance is to bring the first tenth of our increase. Second, the Israelites brought their tithe to the place of worship to honor God. Giving to a charity certainly helps others in need, but it is not a replacement for tithes which expresses your heart for God by following His instruction. Third, tithing requires an attitude of gratefulness and praise, acknowledging God first above all else, and giving abundantly because of the abundance God provides for us every day. This refers to not only an abundance in the form of finances but through the blessings we take for granted that allow us to function daily. *Tithes and offerings were brought abundantly to the house of the Lord* (2 Chronicles 31:4-5,11-12).

Certainly, we can share our income with various organizations and ministries that support the needs of others. But God has a special place in His heart for the church (Ephesians 5:25b; Psalm 73:1) for whom He shall return (Matthew 24:27; 1 Thessalonians 4:16-17). He wants us to help one another but most of all support the household of faith (Galatians 6:6-10). He loves to specifically bless those whom He has set apart in His service. *"Those that be planted in the house of the Lord shall flourish in the courts of our God"* (Psalm 92:13).

Why A Tenth? The only valuation I could find throughout the Scriptures concerning tithes is a tenth of the Israelite's increase to be given to God for the descendants of Levi. For instance, Numbers 18:21,24 says, *"[21]And, behold, I have given the children of Levi all the tenth in Israel for an inheritance, for their service which they serve, even the service of the tabernacle of the congregation. [24]"... the tithes of the children of Israel, which they offer as an heave offering unto the Lord, I have given to the Levites to inherit: ..."*

Leviticus 27:30,32 also mentions, *"[30]And all the tithe of the land; whether of the seed of the land, or of the fruit of the tree, is the Lord's: it is holy unto the Lord. [32]And concerning the tithe of the herd, or of the flock, even of whatsoever passeth under the rod, the tenth shall be holy unto the Lord."* The tenth is a sacred measurement established by God because He is holy. It is a benchmark for tithes today, an amount that we know God approves of and thus we can commit to Him without adding to or taking away from His Word (Deuteronomy 4:2). The significance of tithing continues today because the Word of God will continue forever (Isaiah 40:8).

Should you start tithing or continue to tithe? The decision to tithe is between you and God. I am only providing references to God's Word that I pray will be instrumental in your decision. When I consider the Biblical content that I have studied to write this blog, I believe that Christ fulfilled the initial "purpose" of the law. This purpose originally held us accountable unto death based on our obedience to the laws of God (Deuteronomy 8:11-20). In fulfilling the requirement, He gave us a new covenant by placing the laws on our hearts and writing them in our minds (Hebrews 10:16). Now we will always remember His sacrifice and how God wants us to live. His new covenant teaches us to love God completely and love others as ourselves. When we completely and unconditionally love as God commanded us to love, we learn to follow Christ Who is the only One capable of following God's commands perfectly.

Even today, moral and certain civil laws that we practice are influenced by the laws God commanded. Ceremonial laws, such as communion and water baptism, are practiced in remembrance of Jesus' sacrifice, and as a public acknowledgement of accepting His precious gift of salvation. Yet the commandment of tithing which would support the church and the well-being of those in need is always up for question. Why? Maybe tithing is such an issue because today it consists of money, unlike the agricultural or livestock tithes required in Biblical times.

Today we tend to value money over any other possession because for some people it is hard to come by, and for others, it is the key to their fulfillment—at least that is what they choose to believe. You can always measure your love for God when you have to choose between funds and faith, which challenges your commitment to God. Choose wisely, and *"Be*

BLESSINGS IN BLOGS: Living Effectively

not deceived; God is not mocked: for whatsoever a man soweth, that shall he also reap" (Galatians 6:7).

As mentioned before in Malachi 3:10, God wants us to bring our tithes into the storehouse (the house of God). Remember, the physical aspect of the church is not most significant. Jacob laid his head on a stone he used for a pillow that he had set up for a pillar at a place he named Bethel—which means the house of God. This was the place where the Lord spoke to him in a dream about his destiny (Genesis Chapter 28). His devotion was all about honoring God who faithfully provided for him. In doing so, he vowed to give a tenth of all that God gave him (Genesis 28:22).

If you are currently not connected with a Bible-based church where you can bring your tithes, pray that God will lead you to a growing church in your area, where prioritizing God and developing disciples is evident by the *"fruit they produce"* (Matthew 7:20). In essence, a growing church is made up of a body of believers in Christ who are taught the Word of God, how to apply it, and how to teach others who will teach others and so on. Until then, continue studying God's Word and pray for guidance, wisdom, and understanding. With your finances, time, and talents, offer support to other ministries who are assisting those who are in need while you are searching for a church home. Many Christian radio stations and other Bible-based ministries of faith—local, national, and abroad—are making a significant impact in leading the unsaved[7] to Christ. They are a great source of spiritual support while individuals seek to find the church where they can connect and serve as a body of believers.

Final Thoughts About Tithes. Jesus answered the Pharisees regarding the special tax levied to non-Roman citizens, *". . . Render therefore unto Caesar the things which are Caesar's; and unto God the things that are God's* (Matthew 22:15-22; Mark 12:13-17; Luke 20:20-26). Basically, even today, there are two ways we spend money, by force and by desire. For example, look at the deductions on your pay stub. By force you pay taxes and Social Security. By desire you may choose to pay for health insurance and other benefits that you value.

Page | 161

What bothers people the most about tithing? Is it the amount, the lack of understanding that it already belongs to God (Leviticus 27:30), or the lack of faith that God will keep us from falling financially? Jesus said *"²⁵ . . . Take no thought for your life, what ye shall eat, or what ye shall drink; nor yet for your body, what ye shall put on. Is not the life more than meat, and the body than raiment? ²⁶Behold the fowls [birds] of the air: for they sow not, neither do they reap, nor gather into barns; yet your heavenly Father feedeth them. Are ye not much better than they?"* (Matthew 6:25,26). How much more does God have to give before we stop placing a greater value on a portion of our increase? In the process of deciding whether or not to tithe, people also wonder whether to tithe a tenth from their gross or net income. How can we even ask such a question when the government imposes taxes on our gross income? The question we should ask ourselves is "who is greater, God or government?"

Giving tithes is an expression of faith that God will supply all our needs (Philippians 4:19). When we tithe, we are saying that God means so much more than the tenth that we choose to give back to Him. When we place God above all else, the tenth of our increase becomes an automatic response not by force as with taxes; but by our love for Christ, our faith in God, and the desire to please Him. For *". . . without faith it is impossible to please him; for he that cometh to God must believe that he is, and that he is a rewarder of them that diligently seek him"* (Hebrews 11:6). As with salvation, we have a choice whether or not to tithe. We either tithe or we don't. Choose wisely.

Comments | About Tithing

Why Aren't We There Yet?

CHRISTIANS WHO FEEL like they aren't living the abundant life God promised sometimes feel overwhelmed and anxious (Philippians 4:6). What allows us to reach our goals to fulfill the hope that lies within us is to keep pressing forward without looking back (Philippians 3:13,14). As we grow from childhood to adulthood we develop certain expectations in life. Yet, when life happens, we find ourselves on a path full of uncertainties. As a result, we may start to doubt our abilities or wonder if we should even continue trying. Such a winding road to our desired destination can make us ask ourselves, *"Why aren't we there yet?"*

Not everyone goes through this, but for those who do, there is hope. First, know that you are not alone. Many people go through this phase. What's most important is that you don't stay there. Second, start believing that you will definitely move forward because you have already made progress. You just can't see it yet. Christ opened the door for achievement when He victoriously fulfilled God's plan for salvation (1 Corinthians 15:1-4). *". . . Thus it is written, and thus it behoved Christ to suffer, and to rise from the dead the third day:"* (Luke 24:46). Christ completed the work

He was sent to Earth to do as God had planned. That's just it, we can see our achievements if we view them based on God's plan, outlined in His Holy Word. Achieving is not necessarily finishing in the way we expect. God reveals all that we need to know to advance to the next phase of our journey. Therefore, we can't get stuck in one phase and give up just because we don't know the outcome.

Consider this: suppose God gives us the entire plan from the start. We might forget something, cut corners, or run the other way (Jonah 1:1-3). Generally, when God reveals the initial part of His plan, our minds automatically try to fill in the blanks. Then, when we think we have it all figured out, the plan changes. Or does it? No, it doesn't change at all. The plan continues to unfold exactly the way God intended. All of a sudden we start doubting whether we will be able to successfully complete the task. We may even wonder if we heard God in the first place. Suddenly we are discouraged and feel like giving up. But remember, a successful outcome is not about finishing the task in the way we initially envisioned. It is simply completing the task in the way the task is written.

God wrote the plan for our lives and He will see that we complete the race that He has set before us (Hebrews 12:1). He starts us out with an initial idea and points us in the right direction. He simply asks us to start moving forward, keeping His Word in our hearts and minds. We don't know exactly how we'll get to the finish line, and we don't even know when we will actually finish. All we are to do is keep moving forward and trusting the Lord to guide us along the way. Likewise, stop trying to get ahead of God (Ecclesiastes 9:11), just move at a steady pace and keep Christ first.

Don't worry about how or when you will arrive. When God's plan is your main priority in life, He will keep you moving in the right direction to arrive on time. If you get a little anxious and veer off the path a bit, God will guide you back on course as long as you listen to His correction (Proverbs 3:11-12). You may encounter a few bruises as you try to hold on when things get a little rough or overwhelming, but you'll survive because *God never fails* and *with God all things are possible* (Zephaniah 3:5 and

Matthew 19:26). He even places the right people and resources in your life at the right times to keep you encouraged. But remember to worship God (our Provider) not the provisions. They are blessings to sustain you as you follow Christ. He wants to see you fulfill the plans that He has for you (Jeremiah 29:11). Running your race crying and complaining about it taking too long or not going the way you expect will only slow you down. Be glad it is not going your way! Have you ever thought about what God may be protecting you from by not meeting your expectations?

God's plan is outlined in His Holy Word. Read your Bible for His instructions (2 Timothy 3:16) so life won't take you by surprise. Become familiar with God's Word (2 Timothy 2:15) and start applying it to your life today. Then you will understand how much God loves you and that He wants you to be victorious. If you are wondering why you aren't there yet, make sure you are working on God's plan and in God's time.

Comments | Why Aren't We There Yet?

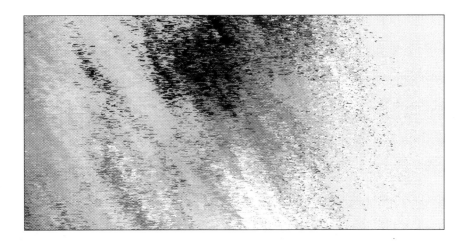

While We Wait

The world is like a classroom of children left to follow instructions in the teacher's absence. Throughout elementary school all of my teachers were female until after my 5th grade year. In general, most children spend a significant part of their day under the instruction of their teacher and the influence of classmates. So naturally I felt more comfortable around an instructor who represents the icon of a mother—one who is able to teach with a nurturing, patient, and caring spirit and who would equitably maintain order among the siblings. But when I was promoted to the 6th grade, my whole perspective of a teacher went right out the window like the eyes of a day-dreaming student.

On the first day of school, a man named Mr. Williams entered the classroom. I remember wondering, "Why was he here?" "Did he come to tell us that our real teacher will be late?" No. Instead, he placed his belongings on the teacher's desk and, after introducing himself, he began the first lesson. I wasn't sure why this unexpected change didn't seem as awkward as I would have thought had we been told ahead of time. But for some reason this teacher seemed worth giving a chance. I have to admit, his style of teaching seemed to keep everyone's interest and was kind of fun too. I was even surprised by his response when I raised my hand for a hall pass to get a drink of water. With no hesitation, rough remarks, or mean expression as I was expecting, he handed me the pass and simply told me to be sure to come right back (Psalm 84:11). When it was time to go home, to my surprise, I was actually looking forward to the next day in his class.

One morning Mr. Williams told us that he would have to leave three hours early. He also said the teachers across the hall would check on us from time to time. Then he wrote complete instructions on the chalkboard so we wouldn't forget what we were supposed to do (Exodus 24:12). Finally, he promised that he would return in the morning (Matthew 16:27,28; 2 Peter 3:12,13).

By now, Mr. Williams knew each student's personality (Luke 12:7). He knew which ones would behave and follow instructions and he knew which ones would rebel. I trusted Mr. Williams and I wanted to follow his instruction because I had learned that he always had everything under control (Psalm 103:19) and our best interest at heart. But as soon as he left, his instructions were no longer a concern for the trouble-makers of the class (Proverbs 26:12). Though I knew the other teachers were there if we needed them, and I knew Mr. Williams said he would return, I also knew that not everyone in our classroom was willing to uphold his requests in his absence. Mr. Williams may have been hoping for 100 percent cooperation (1 Timothy 2:3,4), but some of the students saw this as an opportunity to do whatever they wanted, and they did.

Just as soon as he left, one of the students wasted no time taking charge of the class. He coerced a few others to join him (1 Peter 5:8) and they started distracting and threatening other students as they claimed their new territory. They just wanted to do their own thing and didn't care what would happen when our teacher returned. Because Mr. Williams wasn't physically in the room, they saw no reason to do what he asked or expected. They didn't want to follow the instructions Mr. Williams left on the board and certainly didn't want anyone to remind them of how they should behave. Being in class with them acting this way was quite a challenge. They didn't feel like working and they didn't want anyone else to either. Their defiant behavior affected the other students in the class and they didn't care. The class was divided. Some students gave in and followed the disruptive behavior of those who chose to rebel, while others chose to stand firm (Ephesians 6:14; 2 Thessalonians 2:15) on Mr. Williams' instructions regardless of the apparent distractions.

It wasn't easy, but those of us who chose to wait patiently and continue with the assignment knew that when he would return, we would be better students for our faithfulness and commitment. Though some of the class tried to make us believe that Mr. Williams would never come back, we knew he would (Mark 11:22), and we wanted him to be proud of us for following his instruction and trusting his promise to return. We remained focused while we waited and continued to set an example for others.

> " *12Wherefore, my beloved, as ye have always obeyed, not as in my presence only, but now much more in my absence, work out your own salvation with fear and trembling [be obedient]. 13For it is God which worketh in you both to will and to do of his good pleasure [His purpose for you]. 14Do all things without murmurings and disputing [complaining]: 15 That ye may be blameless and harmless, the sons of God, without rebuke, in the midst of a crooked and perverse nation, among whom ye shine as lights in the world;"* (Philippians 2:12-15).

Comments | While We Wait

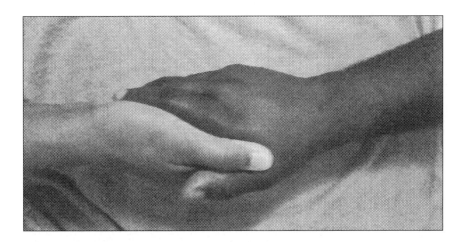

Together As One

EPHESIANS 5:25-27 GIVES a beautiful analogy of Christ's love for the church. This love was demonstrated throughout Biblical history by the grace that God showed towards the Israelites, those whom He chose and loved (Deuteronomy 7:6-9). Time after time, God spared their lives despite their disobedience. Even today, God's love for His people (the church) never fails (1 Corinthians 13:8). The church, the *apple of God's eye*, is the light of the world (Matthew 5:14)—the people God called into a relationship through Christ to share His Gospel of Salvation with others so they may also be saved[5].

The Physical Building. Many people visualize the physical building when referring to the church—a *place* where individuals and families come together with a common focus to reverence God and sing His praises as one in the presence of the Lord. *"Lift up your hands in the sanctuary, and bless the Lord"* (Psalm 134:2). The church building is a *place* where the Word of God is taught to *the saved*[6] (Romans 10:9-10) who seek spiritual growth; and taught to *the unsaved*[7] (2 Corinthians 4:4) who seek to start a relationship with Christ. It is also where we learn how to apply Biblical principles and learn more effective ways to help the unsaved[7] come to the knowledge of Jesus Christ. The church is the house of God, "... *the pillar and ground of the truth*" (1 Timothy 3:15). Though the physical building provides a *place* where we can gather and worship the Lord (Psalm 35:18); we must never confuse its purpose. God's church (the physical building) is instrumental in helping God's church (His children) carry the ministry of Jesus Christ (His mission) into the world.

The Family of God. Members of the church are brothers and sister in Christ (Philippians 1:27b, 3:16b), members of the family of God. Through Christ we have a vertical relationship with God (1 Timothy 2:5) and a horizontal relationship with each other (Hebrews 2:11). As with any family or relationship, the unity within the body of Christ is sometimes challenged by personalities, preferences, and problems that the members may face when interacting. While we are collectively committed to the same cause (Philippians 1:27b) it is crucial that we stay focused on the Word of God to remain *a strong body of believers*—effective learners and followers of Christ. Unity provides a loving and productive atmosphere of worship and praise in the presence of the Lord. We will sustain productive relationships if we function together as one (Philippians 2:2), apply the Word of God to fulfill the purpose of our calling, and avoid getting caught up in religious routines and rituals of worship, losing sight of what God intended for the church (Acts 17:22-34). Essentially, we represent Christ wherever we go (2 Corinthians 5:20). Therefore, our actions and our conversations must represent Christ at all times.

The Body of Christ. Though the church functions as the body of Christ, it is made up of imperfect people, perfected by Christ (Romans 3:23; Ephesians 6:12,13; Matthew 5:48). As we seek to strengthen our relationships we must also keep our bodies healthy and strong since *our bodies are God's temple* (1 Corinthians 3:16)—*the dwelling place of the Holy Spirit whom we have received from God* (1 Corinthians 6:19).

Engaging in habits that are harmful to the body such as smoking, overeating or excessively drinking intoxicating beverages compromises the property of God. Even insufficient rest is harmful to the body. *"It is vain [useless] for you to rise up early, to sit up late, . . . for so he giveth his beloved sleep"* (Psalm 127:2). These harmful practices can break down the body and result in an ineffective witness for Christ. *"And whatsoever ye do in word or deed, do all in the name of the Lord Jesus, giving thanks to God and the Father by him"* (Colossians 3:17). If we follow Christ as our example, we become better examples for others (1 Thessalonians 1:6,7; 1 Timothy 4:12). We also set an example when we demonstrate our love for Christ by the way we treat each other.

Worship Together. Because our bodies are the temple of God who dwells within us, we can worship God anywhere anytime. No matter where we are, we represent Christ; not only in the church building, but in our homes, at our place of employment, *everywhere.* Does this mean that we have to walk around quoting Scriptures all the time? No. The way in which we live and interact with others is how we effectively represent Christ, yet we must always be ready to share God's Word when He presents the opportunity. In this, we know that it is God's will and our efforts will be effective. *"So shall my word be that goeth forth out of my mouth: it shall not return unto me void [empty], but it shall accomplish that which I [God] please, and it shall prosper in the thing whereto I [God] sent it"* (Isaiah 55:11).

Nonetheless, coming to the church, the physical facility, not only allows us to worship God in unity, but also gives us an opportunity to step away from our everyday environments and out of our regular routines to give God our undivided attention. Together we are *"the body of Christ, the fullness of Him that filleth all in all"* (1 Corinthians 12:27-31; Ephesians 1:23), the unified body of believers for whom Christ will return (Matthew 24:27; 1 Thessalonians 4:16-17). We are the eyes that see the forgotten, the arms that embrace the broken, the voice that encourages the hopeless, and the feet that run to serve— *"For we are labourers together with God:..."* (1 Corinthians 3:9a).

While the members of the church work together, they become an even stronger multi-talented family of God. *"21 In whom all the building fitly framed together groweth unto an holy temple in the Lord: 22 In whom ye also are builded together for an habitation of God through the Spirit"* (Ephesians 2:21,22). Just as there are all kinds of people in our earthly family, each with different hopes, dreams, and God-given abilities, there are all kinds of people who make up the family of God. These are individuals who continue to learn and produce spiritual fruit (results) to further the kingdom of God. Though the church family is made up of individuals that most likely have no other common bond, God commands us to love one another unconditionally (John 13:34,35), just as Christ loves the church (Ephesians 5:25b). *"For as we have many members in one body, and all members have not the same office: So we, being many, are one body in Christ, and every one members one of another"* (Romans 12:4,5).

It is a privilege to come together and worship the Lord in a public setting—growing spiritually to effectively carry out God's plan. We are most effective when we utilize the gifts God has given us to edify[2] the body of Christ (1 Corinthians 12:12,27-28). Every member is important to the entire body in order for the church to fulfill the vision God has given the spiritual leader (pastor)—for *"Where there is no vision, the people perish: . . ."* (Proverbs 29:18). If the church starts to veer away from the vision of God by incorporating worldly influences or the personal preferences of a prominent few, some of the members may become discouraged, frustrated, or choose to disconnect from the church. As a result, the members that depart look for another church home or give up all together and resort to independent Bible study.

Those who are committed to independent Bible study sometimes supplement their study with materials written by Christian authors and online research. Studying the Bible independently is essential for spiritual growth and personal development, but the individual disconnected from the church forgoes receiving the blessing of the message God inspires the pastor or minister to deliver. This individual will also miss out on the opportunity to impact the lives of others who are present in the congregation.

Every member of the church has a specific purpose as well as a collective responsibility to love and support one another in order to function effectively. Ephesians 4:4,11-13,22,24,32 tells us that,

> "⁴There is one body, and one Spirit, even as ye are called in one hope of your calling. ¹¹And he gave some, apostles; and some, prophets; and some, evangelists; and some, pastors and teachers; ¹²For the perfecting [equipping] of the saints, for the work of the ministry, for the edifying² of the body of Christ: ¹³Till we all come in the unity of the faith, and of the knowledge of the Son of God, unto a perfect man, unto the measure of the stature of the fullness of Christ: ²²That ye put off concerning the former conversation the old man, which is corrupt according to the deceitful lusts; ²⁴And that ye put on the new man, which after God is created in righteousness and true holiness. ³²And be ye kind one to another, tenderhearted, forgiving one another, even as God for Christ's sake hath forgiven you."

Celebrate Christ. Contrary to what some people may believe, living each day for Christ is not a chore or a boring waste of time, but rather the kind of effort we would put forth to prepare for a grand celebration. As with any celebration, when we receive the invitation of the Lord (Revelation 3:20; Matthew 11:28; John 7:37) we must first accept it (Romans 10:9,10) before we can come into the presence of the One who is celebrated (Psalm 107:8,32). We are always excited to organize or attend celebrations that honor those whom we feel are worthy because we have seen their accomplishments or contributions. However, not everything of value is visible. The blessings we receive from the Lord may not always provide a physical benefit, but they are far greater than anything we strive to achieve on our own. Even then our efforts are attributed to the Lord who gives us the strength to accomplish what we desire (Deuteronomy

8:17,18). Remember, the Lord deserves our greatest adoration. He is honored when we come together as one to celebrate Him.

God's Spoken Word. Through God's spoken Word we are blessed, whereby the hearts of those who are saved[5] are strengthened (Psalm 73:26) and the eyes of the unsaved[7] are opened (Psalm 119:18). The spoken Word of God is intended to be heard as the congregation comes together to worship God collectively and to edify[2] one another (Romans 14:18,19; 1 Thessalonians 5:11) as one body of believers in Christ. The focus of the church is to teach the Word of God and develop the members as disciples (learners) who are committed to building up the body of Christ.

Gone are the days when believers only expect the pastor to shout a good sermon and the choir to sing their favorite song. Believers today are hungry for the Word of God. They want to know, for instance, the background of the Biblical writers, the culture, and the principles of Jesus' teachings. They want to know how the Word of God applies to their lives and what they can do to live more effectively for Christ. Spiritual maturity is hindered if believers are only given the milk of the Word as a babe in Christ (1 Peter 2:2), unable to digest the meat of God's Word (1 Corinthians 3:1-3) and walk in the life God intended.

Remember, *"Ye are the salt of the earth: but if the salt have lost his savour, wherewith shall it be salted? It is thenceforth good for nothing, but to be cast out, and to be trodden under foot of men"* (Matthew 5:13). Salt has a one of a kind, irreplaceable flavor. Like salt, we are the unique seasoning God uses to bring out the flavor of His Word. The Word of God is food for the spirit that sustains life for the believer. *"Every word of God is pure: he is a shield unto them that put their trust in him"* (Proverbs 30:5).

God speaks to us in many ways, for instance, through the Scriptures we read, in our spirit, in a song, or through those whom He has called to teach (Jeremiah 3:15; Isaiah 52:7; Proverbs 11:30). Through their obedient response to His calling, God enables them to spread the Gospel for the edification (the uplifting) of the body of Christ. *"[15]And how shall they preach, except they be sent? As it is written, How beautiful are the feet of them that preach the gospel of peace, and bring glad tidings of good things!* [17]*So then faith cometh by hearing, and hearing by the word of God"* (Romans 10:15, 17). Only those who are called by God are equipped to lead and teach the body of believers.

The Apostle Paul was previously named Saul, a Jewish tentmaker with Roman citizenship who persecuted Christians prior to his conversion. He was later known as Paul when he was appointed by God to preach to the Gentiles (Acts 9:1-20; 13:9) In Ephesians 3:8-9, Paul, with humility, expressed *that he is given the grace to preach to the Gentiles the unsearchable riches of Christ, and to make plain to everyone the fellowship of this mystery, which from the beginning of the world has been hid in God, who created all things by Jesus Christ.*

Just think of the blessing the multitudes in Biblical times would have missed if they stayed at home to study rather than gather together at the feet of Jesus to hear the Word of God. When God calls a pastor [minister/ teacher] to speak the message that He has given, it is in our best interest to be present to listen. Independent study is very important to reinforce our Biblical knowledge, allowing us to better understand what we hear in a sermon. But coming to the church to hear the sermon is just as important, as it also reinforces what we have studied. Hearts are changed and lives are saved at the sound of God's spoken Word, as with those in response to Peter's sermon in Acts 2:34-41. Peter was an Apostle, one of the twelve disciples who walked with Christ. A portion of his sermon is as follows:

[34]*For David is not ascended into the heavens: but he saith himself, The Lord said unto my Lord, Sit thou on my right hand,* [35]*Until I make thy foes thy footstool.* [36]*Therefore let all the house of Israel know assuredly, that God hath made that same Jesus, whom ye have crucified, both Lord and Christ.* [37]*Now when they heard this, they were pricked in their heart, and said unto Peter and to the rest of the apostles, Men and brethren, what shall we do?* [38]*Then Peter said unto them, Repent, and be baptized every one of you*

in the name of Jesus Christ for the remission of sins, and ye shall receive the gift of the Holy Ghost. [39]For the promise is unto you, and to your children, and to all that are afar off [generations to come], even as many as the Lord our God shall call. [40]And with many other words did he testify and exhort, saying, Save yourselves from this untoward [crooked] generation. [41]Then they that gladly received his word were baptized: and the same day there were added unto them about three thousands souls.

The people that heard Peter's sermon were blessed to receive such a powerful life changing message. *"[44]And all that believed were together, and had all things common; [46]And they continued daily with one accord in the temple, and breaking bread from house to house, did eat their meat with gladness and singleness of heart, [47]Praising God, and having favor with all the people. And the Lord added to the church daily such as should be saved"* (Acts 2:44, 46-47).

God's wisdom is made known through the preaching and teaching of His spoken Word. It is extended to all who will gather to listen and learn so that the Word of God may be fulfilled (Luke 4:14-21). Thus it is beneficial for us to connect with a local Bible-teaching church to hear the Word of God as it is given to those who are called to preach and teach; and to worship and praise the Lord as one. *"Praise ye the Lord. I will praise the Lord with my whole heart, in the assembly of the upright, and in the congregation"* (Psalm 111:1). *"Let them exalt him also in the congregation of the people, and praise him in the assembly of the elders"* (Psalm 107:32). The spoken Word of God can reassure God's promise in the hearts of the saved[5] and reveal God's purpose in the minds of the unsaved[7] to bring them to the saving knowledge of Christ.

Women Pastors? The office of a church pastor is based on the Word of God. *"[God] put all things under the feet of Christ, and made Him the head over all things to the church"* (Ephesians 1:22). The debate of whether women should be permitted to pastor a church continues even today.

Those who strongly oppose base their stance on 1 Corinthians 14:34-35: *"³⁴Let your women keep silence in the churches: for it is not permitted unto them to speak; but they are commanded to be under obedience, as also saith the law. ³⁵And if they will learn any thing, let them ask their husbands at home: for it is a shame for women to speak in the church."* However, keep in mind, when studying the Scriptures in the Bible, under the guidance of The Holy Spirit who directs us into all truth (John 16:13), the culture, the times, and the teachings of Christ must be considered. I certainly have my own opinion about this; however, I believe it is best to stay within the boundaries of God's perspective. *"Be of the same mind one toward another. Mind not high things, but condescend to men of low estate. Be not wise in your own conceits [proud notions]"* (Romans 12:16).

Before the birth of Christ, women were not allowed to study the Law, speak or actively participate in the synagogue; basically they were restricted to domestic concerns. Yet contrary to the custom of Jews and Greeks of Biblical times, Jesus' ministry included women. For instance, women were present when Jesus fed and taught the multitudes (Matthew 14:13-21; Mark 6:30-44). Jesus commended Mary for prioritizing His teachings (Luke 10:38-42), and on several occasions He spoke publicly with women (Matthew 9:20-22; Matthew 15:22) which was definitely unacceptable according to Jewish and Greek customs. Even more interesting, women were the first to proclaim The Good News of Jesus Christ (Matthew 28:10).

Anyone still holding to 1 Corinthians 14:34-35 as their reason for opposing women pastors refuses to see that the Scripture does not specifically say that women cannot hold the office of the pastor. The Apostle Paul in 1 Timothy 2:12 says *"But I suffer [permit] not a woman to teach, nor to usurp authority over the man, but to be in silence."* Before the manifestation of Christ, somehow while stressing over the law, religious leaders started developing their own version of the law to fit the customs of the times.

The peculiar thing about this entire debate, whether or not women should be allowed to hold the office of pastor, is that those opposing contradict what they are determined to uphold when they allow women to teach a class. Those opposing women pastors stand firmly by the Scripture, Timothy 2:12. Are women silent in the church? No. They are actively involved in various areas of ministry, utilizing their God-given talents for the glory of God. Besides, Paul may have been referring to *certain* women of that time period, not necessarily all women. Acts 18:18 tells how Paul allowed Priscilla and her husband Aquila to accompany him during his ministry. When Priscilla and Aquila heard Apollos (a great teacher instructed in the way of the Lord) speak boldly in the synagogue, they furthered his knowledge by teaching him the way of salvation because at the time he only knew the baptism of John (Acts 18:24-26). Other women also supported Paul's ministry whom he highly recommended for service in the church (Romans 16:1-4). Priscilla and Aquila also taught in their home, of which Paul commended the church to accept as a viable ministry (Romans 16:5). In addition, Paul gave recognition to Mary's support in the ministry as well (Romans 16:6).

I totally agree that men should step up and become more visible and lead in the church as they are to be visible in their homes and lead their families. For instance, as Paul describes the office of the bishop in 1 Timothy, Chapter 3, he emphasizes in verse 5 that a man who leads in the church must know how to lead his own family. Still, we should never reject whomever God calls to preach and teach His Word. We should never restrict or reject the gifts of the Holy Spirit (1 Thessalonians 5:19) that God intended to benefit the body of Christ. No one has the authority to judge whether or not someone, male or female, is called by God to teach or hold the office of a pastor.

This debate is just one of many distractions to keep the church from functioning effectively. Those who truly love God follow Christ, who demonstrated His incredible love for us through His suffering, death, burial and resurrection. This was a love that no one else could ever offer because only Christ was capable of victoriously delivering us from the enemy (Satan). *"[11]For the Lord has redeemed Jacob, and ransomed him from the hand of him that was stronger than he. [12]Therefore they shall come and sing in the height of Zion, and shall flow together to the goodness of the Lord . . . and their soul shall be as a watered garden; they shall not sorrow any more at all"* (Jeremiah 31:11-12). As for pastors, male or female, what matters most is whether they are called by God and faithfully serve Him.

New Believers in Christ. When new believers unite with a church they become a viable member of the body of Christ. As the church continues to grow there are many opportunities for them to utilize their God-given talents, treasures, and time to support the ministry God has established through the church. A common misconception of new believers is that they receive salvation by joining a church. However, salvation is only received through Jesus Christ. Jesus said *". . . I am the way, the truth, and the life: no man cometh unto the Father, but by me [Christ]* (John 14:6). Through the grace of God we are saved (Ephesians 2:8,9) not by our works, and not by church membership. Romans 10:9 says, if you *confess the Lord Jesus and believe in your heart that God raised him from the dead you are saved.* By accepting Jesus Christ as your Lord and Savior, you are committing to a life in Christ, a life that is acceptable and pleasing to God.

Once you receive Christ as your Lord and Savior, you are adopted into the *family of God.* Whether or not you remain a member of the church where you publically confessed your new relationship in Christ, your membership in the *family of God* is forever. You may choose to change your church membership, but transferring does not affect your salvation which is everlasting. According to John 3:16, *"For God so loved the world, that he gave his only begotten Son, that whosoever believeth in him should not perish, but have everlasting life."* When God says that you will have everlasting life you can lean on His promise because He never fails (1 Chronicles 28:20b; Zephaniah 3:5). This is all the more reason to spend your time on Earth learning to serve the Lord by doing what is pleasing to God (Hebrews 11:6). Nothing in this world is guaranteed, but knowing that our salvation is sure is the greatest blessing anyone could ever receive.

With such a priceless gift, we should be excited about coming together to honor God as one big family. The first epistle (letter) of Peter, Chapter 2 verse 5 describes the church as God's spiritual house in that, *"Ye also, as lively stones, are built up a spiritual house, an holy priesthood, to offer up spiritual sacrifices, acceptable to God by Jesus Christ."* Christ is the foundation and cornerstone. Like the stone the builders rejected, Christ is the greatest of the house of God (1 Peter 2:6-8). Those who are connected to the body of Christ collectively *show the praises of Him who has called us out of darkness into His marvelous light* (1 Peter 2:9).

Thousands of years ago God led and protected a nation with whom He found favor and later extended His grace to the entire world (1 John 2:1,2). Throughout the Bible, God demonstrates His desire to unify the people He refers to as the church, whom He continuously blesses. *"13 Those that be planted in the house of the Lord shall flourish in the courts of our God"* (Psalm 92:13). To honor the amazing love He has shown towards us we worship Him with grateful hearts and adoration. *"52 And they worshipped him [Jesus Christ], and returned to Jerusalem with great joy: 53 And were continually in the temple, praising and blessing God. Amen"* (Luke 24:52,53). May the church continually praise and worship our Lord together as one.

Comments | Together As One

God Answers Prayer

WHEN I PLAN, I always pray! Why? Because every now and then, for whatever reason, my plans seem to totally go in a different direction. Prayer helps see me through the course of uncertainty. Occasionally life brings new challenges or unexpected changes—something thrown into the mix that you just didn't see coming; and all you can do is keep moving forward.

Though I prayed before I got out of bed this morning, the minute I sat down to my desk at the office I still couldn't avoid the distractions that followed. It's not that my prayer wasn't answered. This was just one of those days. Still, with all that happened, the obstacles actually created another opportunity for me to look to God (Psalm 46:1).

Basically, this is how my day was destined to unfold. One Thursday morning as soon as I logged onto my computer my boss stepped into my office. He hesitantly asked if I could finish the report he originally requested for Friday by the end of today. I didn't mind the new deadline because I was intending to submit the report a day early anyway. At least that was my plan.

Then, the phone rang. One of my clients called to get the status of another project I was working on and took longer than necessary to recap the details we discussed during our last meeting. Of course, the deadline for her project was also Friday. As I looked down my list of things to do, I tried to stay encouraged (John 16:33) and remind myself that I can get everything done (Philippians 4:13) if I stay focused.

After checking off the few things I had already completed on my weekly agenda, I noticed that it was getting close to lunchtime. Down the hall I heard my coworkers gathering in the breakroom to celebrate employee birthdays for the month. Though not mandatory, the company always encouraged participation in staff events to promote and maintain a team environment. Since I had such a tight deadline and I already brought my lunch from home, I wasn't going to attend until my boss stepped into my office and was waiting for me to go to the breakroom too. How could he do this and expect me to have his report ready by the end of the day? Nevertheless, we went to the break room for the birthday luncheon (1 Thessalonians 5:11). Immediately after the lunch break, I rushed back to my office hoping to complete the report and at least move a little further on the project for my client.

As soon as I had finally refocused on the report, a popup window from my calendar appeared on my screen to remind me of a meeting in the conference room that would start in 10 minutes. I grabbed a notepad, pen, and a printout of my weekly agenda and rushed down the stairs to the conference room so I wouldn't be the last to arrive. Usually the last person to arrive would be the first to give his or her weekly progress report, and I needed a few minutes to make a few updates.

Finally, when I returned to my desk, I opened the report that was due by the end of the day to finish entering the data my boss gave me last week. About two hours later, when I was nearly finished, to my surprise my boss called me into his office to apologize. The data he provided last week was incorrect. My response was *"no problem,"* of course, what else could I say (Proverbs 15:1). As I returned to my desk more anxious about meeting my deadline, I tried to calm down by remembering that whatever

I do, as a believer in Christ, I must do whole-heartedly unto the Lord (Colossians 3:23). So I sat down, reopened the document, and focused on entering the new data from the twenty-five page printout my boss just provided. By the length of this document I knew that my other plans were scratched for the rest of the day. Again, I prayed (1 Thessalonians 5:17) while typing as quickly as possible.

Now fifteen minutes prior to the end of the day, I hadn't entered even half of the new data from the printout. That's when I realized that there was no way I could finish this report today (Matthew 19:26; Mark 10:27; Luke 18:27). Just as I reached to pick up the phone to tell my boss that the report would not be ready until Friday as he originally requested, he sent me an E-mail. I opened it thinking he was going to ask if I had finished, but instead he wrote, *"You know what, the data you had at first was the right data after all. Go ahead and send me what you have so far."*

For a brief moment, I just sat there starring at my computer, realizing that when I started entering the new data, I was in such a hurry, I typed right over the original. That's when an uneasy feeling came over me. So I sat back in my chair, breathed deeply, and kept praying (Psalm 34:4). Then suddenly, I remembered that I saved a copy of the document on my USB (Universal Serial Bus) flash drive as a backup right after the meeting.

Days like this are reminders that no matter how pressing or impossible a task may be, God answers prayer (Matthew 7:7; Mark 11:24; Luke 11:9). We may not see results right away but God always comes through when we really need Him. God allows the Holy Spirit to give us peace (John 14:26,27) while we wait. The Holy Spirit helps hold us together when we feel like everything is falling apart. God is the only One we can call on, even when we feel like He's not listening or seems too far away.

God is greater (Deuteronomy 4:39) than any situation we will ever face. He is way ahead of our timeframe, already working out the issue, because He knows where we are going before we get there. We just have to stay calm (John 14:1), pray, and keep moving until we can catch up to where He is leading us.

All we have to do is trust God and know that He keeps His Word and keeps us moving forward according to His plan (Jeremiah 29:11). We can always "... *call upon Him and He will answer [us] and show [us] great and mighty things which [we] have not known"* (Jeremiah 33:3).

Comments | God Answers Prayer

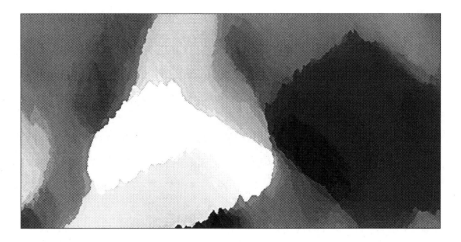

When God Calls, Listen

Earlier in my life, my experience of reading the Bible mainly consisted of: studying with others at church, following a sermon during a worship service, or referencing specific Scriptures to write newsletter articles and other content for Biblical resources. Occasionally I would stop and read a passage independently, mostly during difficult times for encouragement. Basically, I never seemed to have time to read any books or periodicals except for on a need to know basis.

Generally, I would read to teach myself new skills or improve my current abilities. I enjoyed reading to learn a new software program or useful tips for finance, health, and design. I have always had a strong desire to see progress, no matter how small. Thus, I devoted most of my reading to develop my talents. I later realized that reading for self-improvement is only effective when you also read God's Word for spiritual growth. That was when I decided to read the entire Bible in a year.

At first the Bible was very difficult to understand because the King James Version (KJV) was the only Bible I had available at the time. For me it was like reading a foreign language or the writings of Shakespeare.

I prayed for understanding but because I had just begun to explore the Bible from a reader's rather than a researcher's perspective, I needed to give myself time to get familiar with the use of words such as *"thee," "thou," "thy,"* and *"thine,"* or words that end with *"eth."* I thought about reading other versions of the Bible, for instance, the New International Version (NIV), but I was concerned that a contemporary interpretation of the Scriptures may not adequately represent God's truth. Then, when I talked with several ministers and Bible study teachers about contemporary translations, they suggested I try the NIV as a supplement to the KJV. Though the NIV is a translation of the Holy Bible in contemporary English, I still prefer reading the KJV and then cross-referencing the NIV because the KJV was translated prior to the NIV. When I checked the inside front pages of the Holy Bible, KJV and the NIV Life Application Study Bible, I learned that the KJV was originally published in 1611 and the NIV in 1965. Today, there are several versions of the Bible available. While reading other translations, I noticed how some were so different that I wondered if they lost the validity of God's Word. Regardless of our preference, we must all rely on the Holy Spirit for understanding.

Early in my studies, though I was starting to understand some of the meaning behind the Scriptures, I still wasn't connecting to the principles for life application. I read about Biblical events that seemed in my mind too impossible for real people, and several situations that seemed extremely unfair. After many unsuccessful attempts of independent study, skipping days and starting over, I decided to take a different approach.

One evening during a Bible study lesson at a church, a teacher asked, *"How can you trust someone you don't know?"* He was referring to the reason some people have doubts in their relationship with Christ. He had no idea that his question was the answer to my struggle with reading the Bible. Thinking about his question I realized the reason I couldn't connect to the principles was because I really didn't know the Person by which the principles were designed. To know God I needed to know our Lord and Savior Jesus Christ (John 1:1,14; John 7:28,29). I knew from previous Bible study lessons that the Gospels of Matthew, Mark, Luke, and John, the first four books of the New Testament, present the life of Jesus Christ from birth to death. So I decided to start reading the New Testament to learn more about Jesus Christ, our Lord and Savior. I started with the KJV, supplemented by the NIV.

As I learned more about the Lord's character, His purpose, and His unconditional love for mankind, I began to grow in my relationship with Him and wanted to learn even more about Him. The Scriptures suddenly came alive in my mind like a memory of something that I had experienced years ago. I could see what I read so clearly as if I were standing in the midst of each Biblical event. With my yellow highlighter I marked the Scriptures that I could relate to and that provided a message of something I wanted to remember for future reference. Finally, by the end of one year I read the entire KJV of the Bible. For some people, this is no great achievement, but for me it was the difference between a life with Christ and a life in Christ.

The following year, I read the NIV from cover to cover starting with Genesis this time. Since then I have committed to working towards daily reading, either in the morning or during a lunch break. I didn't set a particular amount to read, but I usually tried to read an entire chapter to avoid missing the essence of the Scriptures each chapter contained. Before I would begin to read, I always prayed that the Holy Spirit would provide wisdom and understanding, and guide me as I learn to apply what I read.

Reading the Bible is one way God speaks to us. As we stay focused on His Word, we know when He is calling and all we have to do is listen to follow Him (John 10:27). There have been times in my life when God would speak to my heart, producing the sudden urge for me to read the Bible during times other than my regular routine. Just as we call a family member or friend for something specific, God can call us through the prompting of the Holy Spirit to read the Bible for a specific message He wants to convey at a particular time. Though the Bible was written long ago, the principles of God's Word still applies to today.

Reading the Bible gives me peace and confidence in knowing that God cares and is always with me. Regardless of how urgent things may seem,

I know that God is aware of all my needs and He will respond according to His will and in His perfect time. The more time I spend studying God's Word, the more God's Word becomes clear and applicable to my current situations. Not always immediately or with the entire meaning or purpose revealed, but the principles of God's Word let me know that He is speaking, listening, and moving on my behalf.

Therefore, whenever I have even the slightest urge to pick up my Bible and read it, I will, because God may be trying to tell me something that I need to know for that very moment or for a situation to come. I believe that through the guidance of the Holy Spirit, God reveals a particular scriptural message specifically for a particular time.

I have heard people say that you can't simply open the Bible, turn to a Scripture, and expect to find just what you need to hear or apply to your personal situation at hand. Well, I have to disagree with that notion because God knows exactly what we need and if we listen He will let us know. From experience, I have learned that whenever I respond to the urge to read the Bible beyond my regular daily study, I am blessed. Reading the Bible by the prompting of the Holy Spirit is more than just randomly flipping through the pages. It provides words of encouragement and direction so the Holy Spirit can guide you effectively through life. It also demonstrates obedience to God.

Though there are times when a Scripture doesn't readily seem to relate to a situation, I have experienced instances when the Holy Spirit revealed the purpose of the intervention either immediately or at a later time. One evening, I was struggling to complete a paper for school that was due by midnight. Suddenly I had a strong urge to open my Bible. I really didn't have time to do anything else but to keep working on the assignment; however, I decided to stop, pray, and read anyway because the Word of God should always take precedence over everything else. When I opened the Bible, I turned right to the story of David and Goliath (1 Samuel 17). After reading this very familiar story, I continued writing my paper. While writing I decided to skim the assignment to make sure I was covering all that was required, but then a thought crossed my mind. What if the whole idea of pursuing a Master's degree well into my adulthood is nothing but a waste of time? Well, this negative thought carried some weight until I remembered the chapter I just read from the Bible.

Suddenly I began to see that negative thought as a metaphorical giant of doubt, laughing and saying, "At your age, how can you expect to earn a technical degree with a non-technical background." Remembering how God helped David (who later became king of Judah—2 Samuel 2:1-7) slay the troublesome giant named Goliath of Gath, I was convinced that God can certainly help me defeat my annoying giant of doubt.

The victory of David is very encouraging because it reminds me even today that through faith God gives us the strength and resources to move forward in unlikely situations. The key is to never go into battle with someone else's armor (1 Samuel 17:38-39). In other words, let God prepare you for your specific tasks by allowing Him to speak directly to you when He calls. When you read the Bible and pray for guidance and understanding, God's Word is in your heart for the Holy Spirit to bring back to your remembrance and see you through any situation or circumstance.

During my battle with the giant of doubt, the minute I chose to focus on God's Word and what God has already done, I was able to knock the *giant of doubt* right out of my field of study and *make a homerun!* With God's help I was able to submit my class assignment earlier than the deadline (2 Corinthians 10:3-5). Remember, God is in complete control of everything. Draw upon the things that God has already done in your life to help you continue achieving victories. *"David said . . . , The Lord that delivered me out of the paw of the lion, and out of the paw of the bear, he will deliver me out of the hand of this Philistine. And Saul said unto David, Go, and the Lord be with thee"* (1 Samuel 17:37). Just as God gave David the ability to slay his giant, God will give you the ability to slay your giant. You just have to study the Word of God to know His promises.

Pray and allow the Holy Spirit to guide you into truth and understanding during your personal Bible study. Then you won't go into battle already feeling defeated. You will be able to stand on God's Word as did David, and your victory will glorify God. While facing new challenges and uncertainties, the Holy Spirit will remind you to have faith and confidence in the Lord. The Apostle Paul stated in Philippians 4:13, *"I can do all things through Christ which strengtheneth me [who strengthens me]."* You will know beyond a shadow of a doubt that God's Word *". . . is a lamp onto [your] feet and a light onto [your] path"* (Psalm 119:105). Most of all, *". . . be of good cheer; I have [Christ has] overcome the world"* (John 16:33). The Bible is the voice of God in written form. Read it and let God speak directly to you.

Sharing my experience of personal Bible study is not intended to convince you to flip open your Bible and instantly receive an applicable Scripture of guidance, confirmation, or assurance. Always study the Word of God with purpose, seeking to hear from God what He wants to speak into your life. In addition, be ready to receive a special call that God may make from time to time to keep you encouraged and guide you along the path He has prepared for you. God touches our lives through our faith in Christ and our willingness to listen when He calls.

Comments | When God Calls, Listen

There's Something About Water

> *"⁷For there is hope of a tree, if it be cut down, that it will sprout again, and that the tender branch thereof will not cease. ⁸Though the root thereof wax old in the earth, and the stock thereof die in the ground; ⁹Yet through the scent of water it will bud, and bring forth boughs like a plant"* (Job 14:7-9).

I THINK IT'S interesting how I am more in tune with God spiritually when I spend time in or near water. Though sometimes I write down interesting thoughts when I wake up in the morning, I receive some of the most inspiring ideas when I am around water. I find this true because these are the times when I am least distracted or interrupted. Great ideas or words of encouragement come to mind, for instance, when I am in the shower or washing dishes. Then I can hardly wait to stop and write them down.

I remember when my dishwasher broke. Not that I enjoy housework, but while I washed the dishes I felt a sense of peace as the warm water flowed from the faucet over each dish I held in my hand. Actually, I'm not surprised that such a humbling task provides the perfect time to reflect and receive divine inspiration. Maybe it's the continuous sound of running water that drowns out all other distractions long enough to really listen to God (Psalm 46:3-5).

Around water I am more calm, relaxed, and ready to receive every word God communicates to my heart whenever He speaks. It's not an audible voice that I hear. The words are spoken as thoughts revealed by the Holy Spirit. This is the time I also think about how God has blessed me and how much He has shown His love towards me throughout my life. He reassures me that He will always be with me no matter how difficult times may seem.

One day, I suddenly remembered learning some time ago that a significant percentage of the human body is composed of water. So I started thinking about how God created the world before He created mankind. The Creation of the world in the book of Genesis begins by saying, *"In the beginning God created the heaven and the earth"* (Genesis 1:1). Then I noticed that the first mention of water was at the end of Genesis 1:2, *"And the Spirit of God moved upon the face of the waters."* The last mention of water in the Bible is Revelation 22:17, *"And the Spirit and the bride say, Come. And let him that heareth say, Come. And let him that is athirst come. And whosoever will, let him take the water of life freely."* When I read these Scriptures, I saw that the connection between water and divine inspiration is life. So I continued to search the Scriptures and found several references of water that have a significant impact on life one way or another.

With water, God cleansed the Earth from the sin of humanity[3] when He allowed only Noah and his family to survive a fatal worldwide flood (Genesis Chapter 6 through Chapter 9 verse 17). Water was also evidence of God's Almighty power when He divided the Red Sea so that the Israelites could cross on dry land to freedom (Exodus 14:21). Then He performed this miracle once more so they could cross the Jordan River and enter the Promised Land (Joshua 3:15-17), the land of Canaan. Healing is another Biblical reference of water. Christ healed a lame man at the pool of Bethesda (John 5:1-9), and a blind man at the pool of Siloam (John Chapter 9). Even our tears can contribute to the healing of our sorrows (2 Kings 20:5).

Another reference of water was the miraculous wonder that was witnessed by the disciples of Jesus when He walked on water towards their ship (i.e., boat) (Matthew 14:22-33). Then in response, Peter, one of the disciples, got out of the ship and walked on water towards Jesus (Matthew 14:28,29).

Likewise, there were two life-changing events that took place at a well. A Samaritan women met Jesus and learned of the living water and truth (John 4:7-29). Rebecca who met Abraham's chief servant at the well (Genesis Chapter 24) came to know her destiny. Though there are many Biblical references to water, there is one in particular that has made the greatest impact even today.

Jesus Christ suffered for sins He did not commit (1 Peter 2:21-24). By His excruciating sacrifice (Isaiah 53:3-5) we are given the choice to accept eternal life with Christ. Upon His death before His body was removed from the cross, when one of the soldiers pierced Him in His side with a spear, blood and water flowed from His body (John 19:34). As a result, the power of the Almighty God was confirmed through Christ by two distinct elements: water which signifies life (John 7:37-38) and blood which signifies death (Philippians 2:8; Isaiah 53:5). Through the death, burial, and resurrection of Jesus Christ we are given the gift of eternal life because He is the only Son of the true and living God (Hebrews Chapter 1; 1 Thessalonians 1:9).

By faith we accept Jesus Christ as our Lord and Savior. When He comes into our lives, we are spiritually cleansed and empowered through the baptism of the Holy Spirit (Mark 1:8; John 1:30-33), purified by His presence. We are baptized into Christ and He is within us (Galatians 3:26, 27). After receiving the baptism of the Holy Spirit, we are baptized by water which identifies us with the death, burial, and resurrection of Jesus Christ. Water baptism signifies an everlasting relationship with Christ.

Throughout the Bible God presents many incredible instances where He used water to cleanse, direct, heal, and restore. Certainly there is something about water that cultivates the seed of inspiration. It is life—the life that only God can give.

Comments | There's Something About Water

What Do You See?

WHEN I FIRST read the story of the Apostle Peter walking on water (Matthew 14:22-33) I thought *what an incredible act of faith* (Hebrews Chapter 11). How could that happen and why did it happen to Peter? Only God knows why He chooses certain individuals for certain amazing events. Likewise, only God will allow us to accomplish what seems to be impossible, *for ". . . with God all things are possible"* (Matthew 19:26). So I stopped to think about all the amazing things God has done for me, though there are so much more than this book could contain.

To be able to identify and acknowledge the amazing favor of God in your life, you have to first think about what is your measure of amazement. This declaration may be influenced by your character and your outlook. But most of all, influenced by your relationship with Christ and willingness to see *"the amazing"* in what others may refer to as ordinary. Certainly not every event is intended to be colossal, but what makes it colossal is what it signifies to you.

For some people, receiving a bachelor's degree may not be as impressive as a master's or doctoral degree. But to those who are the first in their family to receive one, it's huge! Likewise, stepping off the curb and making it safely to the other side of the street may not be a big deal. But it is if you just missed a semi-truck speeding through a red light at the same intersection. Still, what's truly colossal is to have faith in Someone you cannot see (John 1:18; 1 John 4:12). Though we worship God in spirit, we are blessed by the results of His love for us every day. While others don't think this is colossal, it is; especially when Christ returns for us, and they are left behind.

With God you can do some amazing things (John 14:12) and have life changing experiences when you choose to see the value these experiences contain by keeping your eyes on Christ. When you focus on the benefit rather than the obstacle, you too will increase your faith as you step out of your boat of uncertainty. If you suddenly feel yourself sinking, remember—all eyes on God, for He is the only One who makes all things possible (Matthew 19:26).

Comments | What Do You See?

Follow God's Perfect Plan

OVER THE YEARS, I have been inspired to move forward with goals that I believed God led me to achieve. Time after time He has opened doors of opportunity, gave me the abilities to handle the challenge, and placed people in my life for encouragement and support. Even so, obstacles always seemed to get in the way making it sometimes difficult to see results. At times the journey was very disappointing and I struggled to keep from feeling like I failed. I even wondered if God had really given me the green light in the first place.

God knows that sometimes we all fall victim to doubt or fear about something. This tendency of uncertainty can lead to procrastination and the decision to abandon the task altogether to reduce losses. Despite what we may think or feel, God's plan prevails (Isaiah 55:11). As long as we follow God's lead He will see us through regardless of any obstacles that try to turn us away. God knows that since we are walking by faith, we tend to grow weak and weary from time to time (Mark 14:38). He doesn't expect us to be perfect but He expects us to follow His perfect plan (Galatians 6:9). Our perfection was stained at the beginning of time when Adam and Eve, the first man and woman God created, sinned against God (Genesis Chapter 3). In our own strength we lack the power and authority to make ourselves perfect again. It is Christ who justifies us (Romans 5:1, Galatians 3:26) through faith. By the grace of God, we are saved (Ephesians 2:8) and brought back into a right relationship with God because of the death, burial and resurrection of Jesus Christ, the only One capable of making such a sacrifice (Acts 4:12).

Though God has given each of us a specific purpose (Ephesians 2:10) with unique abilities, Christ is the only way we are able to accomplish what God calls us to do (John 14:6). Christ is our source of strength even when obstacles get in the way and we feel the load is too heavy to bear. We need Christ to help us follow God's perfect plan to stay encouraged and keep moving forward so not to give into any distractions. God knows that while we are in the flesh we will be distracted from time to time. Jesus recognized this weakness in man when He returned from praying and found that His disciples couldn't stay awake while He was away. He responded by saying, *". . . the spirit indeed is willing but the flesh is weak"* (Matthew 26:41).

God chastises disobedience for spiritual development. He is gracious and merciful enough to love us and help us grow beyond any of our shortcomings. We are reminded of His grace when He said to the afflicted Apostle Paul, *". . . My grace is sufficient for thee, for my strength is made perfect in weakness"* (2 Corinthians 12:9). As a result, we can move forward and accomplish great things for the Lord if we focus on doing God's will (John 6:38) by following His perfect plan. Just as an oven is not designed to preserve food and a refrigerator is not designed to bake, both are effective when functioning exactly as planned.

Comments | Follow God's Perfect Plan

Praise the Lord

EARTH, VERY DRY, gray, randomly broken into pieces, lost, lifeless, and lonely, helpless, hopeless, waiting anxiously for anything that will change the course until finally with a new mind and spirit, placed in a garden that springs forth praise. *"For as the earth bringeth forth her bud, and as the garden causeth the things that are sown in it to spring forth; so the Lord God will cause righteousness and praise to spring forth before all nations"* (Isaiah 61:11)

The Bible clearly tells us that we should not worry or be anxious for anything (Philippians 4:6) because the Lord will raise us up in due time when we humble ourselves, knowing that He cares for us (1 Peter 5:6, 7). Instead, of worrying, *"... PRAISE the Lord, all ye nations: praise him, all ye people. For his merciful kindness is great toward us: and the truth of the Lord endureth for ever. Praise ye the Lord"* (Psalm 117). As we praise the Lord, we put ourselves in the position to be lifted to the life God intended—a life we can truly enjoy that will bring glory to His Name.

"⁵Let the people praise thee, O God; let all the people praise thee. ⁶Then shall the earth yield her increase; and God, even our own God, shall bless us"

(Psalm 67:5,6). When we do not take time to praise the Lord, we miss out on the blessing of worshipping Him; for whether or not we praise Him, *He will be praised* (Luke 19:40).

As we focus on praising the Lord our rocks become precious stones of life—reminding us that we are loved and cherished by God. Always remember that our worth is not in our achievements, but rather in our adoration of God. When we praise the Lord continuously, our hearts and minds are focused on honoring Him (Proverbs 3:9; Colossians 3:17), and we are able to see life from a new perspective. For a new mind and spirit, consider the following:

- *We are here on earth for only a short while* (1 Chronicles 29:15)—*so praise the Lord while there is still time.*
- *Love God with all your heart* (Mark 12:30) *by reverencing, worshipping, and praising Him.*
- *Love others, as you love yourself* (Mark 12:31). *It's ok to love yourself. Then you are able to love others.*
- *Serve God with gladness* (Psalm 100:2), *first above all else because He is worthy.*
- *Serve others to actually benefit them* (Galatians 6:10) *and not for the sake of earning recognition or praise.*
- *Pray to God and know that He hears you and loves you forever* (John 3:16). *Be sure to listen to what He has to say.*
- *Take time to listen to others when they are in need* (Romans 12:10), *even when you don't feel like it or have the time.*
- *Give by faith* (2 Corinthians 9:6,7).
- *Demonstrate confidence in the Lord when no one else will* (Luke 19:40)
- *Have mercy and give grace instead of casting guilt or blame* (Matthew 5:7).
- *Refrain from feeling offended or angry because it is the first and the easiest response* (Ecclesiastes 8:9).
- *Apologize* (Matthew 5:23,24), *whether or not it is accepted .*

- *Forgive, for the sake of your own freedom. But most of all because Christ forgives you* (Ephesians 4:32).
- *Be confident in Christ because of God's unfailing love and promises* (2 Peter 1:4; Titus 1:2).
- *Regardless of how life seems to be, take time to praise the Lord because He is worthy* (Psalm 24).

Comments | Praise the Lord

Action Speaks Louder with the Word

FROM TIME TO time, God allows certain situations to occur in our lives. Though unfavorable, they essentially exist for the purpose of furthering our spiritual growth. Because we naturally try to avoid the uncertainties, how they make us feel immediately becomes our main focus rather than Who is able to see us through. Every situation is uncertain at first, but if we study God's Word and pray for understanding, the Holy Spirit will guide us so that our actions will achieve successful results.

In the midst of a situation, when we struggle feeling sorry for ourselves or question God for allowing this sudden interruption of life, we become distracted and fail to seek God's Word for guidance. Thus, if we are not looking in the right direction for the right solution, we hinder the process of learning from the situation and our voice of action is silenced. What God allows to happen in our lives can only be managed by His instructions because our action speaks louder with the Word of God.

We may know to seek the Lord for direction, but if we never put forth the effort to study and apply His principles to every situation, we cannot expect to move forward in His will. James 1:22 tells us to *be doers of the word and not hearers only.* This means, rather than questioning God's purpose in allowing us to go through a situation, we should trust Him, pray for guidance, and look to the Holy Spirit to lead. By studying God's Word consistently, the Holy Spirit allows us to see our situation in the Light of Truth (John 16:13).

There are many individuals in the Bible from whom God required action on their part in order to accomplish the tasks He called them to fulfill. Some instances that took longer to accomplish than expected (Genesis Chapters 6-7) caused them to operate out of their comfort zone (Numbers Chapter 13), or led them in a direction different than they were accustomed to (The Book of Esther). The choice to follow God's will and act on God's calling was essential to the outcome of each situation. Had they given up completely on God's instruction, they would have forfeited their blessing. Even though God wants us to totally depend on Him, He doesn't want us to be passive and neglect the responsibilities He has given us to fulfill. He wants us to be proactive in following His will, unlike the individual who buried his talent[6] rather than investing it for a greater purpose (Matthew 25:14-30).

Certainly God is pleased when we demonstrate patience, thankfulness, and contentment. The Bible clearly states *"⁶Be careful [anxious] for nothing; but in every thing by prayer and supplication with thanksgiving let your request be made known to God. ⁷And the peace of God, which passeth all understanding, shall keep your hearts and minds through Christ Jesus"* (Philippians 4:6,7). God reminds us that we can make our requests without worrying because He has everything under control. Yet, in our contentment we must not become complacent (independent of God) and hide behind the virtues of satisfaction and gratefulness. Otherwise, we will forego the opportunity to exercise our faith by applying the Word of God.

I can recall difficult times in my life when I wondered if God was telling me to turn around, take another route, or stand still for the moment. Then during my personal time with God as I studied His Word and prayed for understanding, I learned to view the weight of the situation as God's way of testing my commitment and strengthening my faith. The heavier the weight, the more I found myself studying God's Word for strength and endurance. Though God allowed the weight in my life, He never intended for me to carry it alone. He was always right by my side holding me up every step of the way.

Additionally, there were situations where when I prayed, I would wonder if God was listening. Then, when I remembered that Ecclesiastes 3:1 said, *"To every thing there is a season, and a time to every purpose under the heaven,"* I was encouraged to wait for God to respond. God works in His time, not by our expectations. Most of all, God is never late. He knows what we need and when we need Him. Therefore, He does not have to get on our schedule to meet our needs in our timeframe. Nor does He have to rush or make up for lost time because His timing is perfect. We learn to understand and therefore respond to our situations when we become more familiar with God's character as we study His Word. However, when we apply God's Word, we take action according to His will. By following His instructions we are able to move forward in our situation. So, when we study God's Word, pray, and apply what we have learned, we are demonstrating our trust in God by actively seeking His will.

As written in Hebrews 4:16, *"Let us therefore come boldly unto the throne of grace, that we may obtain mercy, and find grace to help in time of need."* When we act in faith according to the Word of God, we can move mountains. *"Jesus answered and said unto them, Verily [truly] I say unto you, If you have faith, and doubt not, ye shall not only do this which is done to the fig tree, but also if ye shall say unto this mountain, Be thou removed, and be thou cast into the sea; it shall be done"* (Matthew 21:21).

Comments | Action Speaks Louder with the Word

SATURDAY, MAY 21, 1:00 P.M.

Blog Bites

(Bite-size spiritual food for thought)

EVERY NOW AND then an interesting thought came to mind that may serve as nuggets of nourishment for spiritual growth.

Almost There. You know you are on the homestretch headed for your breakthrough when you start to experience new issues in your life that suddenly require your attention. Sometimes these events are actually there to distract you from whatever God is leading you to do. It could be a sudden idea or situation that gives you every reason to invest your time and effort, except the most important reason to consider taking action—*you didn't hear this from God.* It could be something you believe you should do to help someone else, but unless you hear from God, don't do it. Remember, God has a plan for your life and He knows exactly what is involved. Though addressing a sudden need may seem to be what will please God and help others, wait for God to give you the authority to move forward.

For every new situation, pray and ask God first if what you believe you should do is in His will. Know how God speaks by studying His Holy Word so you will not be tempted to fall for any distractions. The purpose of a distraction is to throw you off course when you are *almost there*. Why, because you are getting closer to your blessing. The closer you are the more frequent and believable the distraction. The more you read the Bible and pray, the more you will hear what God has to say. When you know God's Word, nothing can get in the way.

Finding Joy. As warm as the word joy sounds, many times it seems to be so distant. It is something just about everyone wants to experience, but can't seem to grasp. Many people think that it is the same as happiness, but joy is not associated with what happens in life. In other words, joy is not merely the product of a great event, a favorable outcome, or accomplished hopes and dreams. Joy is the elated expression of well-being as a result of your willingness to follow God's plan. Furthermore, it is not something that just pops up and says *"I'm here, you can begin feeling great now!"* Joy waits for your invitation because it is based on the love you have for God, others, and even yourself, rather than this earthly life. Like Christ, joy comes when you are willing to receive it and when you are ready to hold on and never let it go.

Who We Really Are. *"I will praise thee; for I am fearfully and wonderfully made: marvellous are thy works; . . ."* (Psalm 139:14). While learning to apply the Word of God, I have come to know that we who are in Christ are so much more than what we may think of ourselves and our experiences of life. We are an amazing creation of God, capable of accomplishing the purpose for which God created us. *"It is God that girdeth me with strength, and maketh my way perfect"* (Psalm 18:32). Despite anyone else's opinion, it is our choice to be the person that God would have us to be as we continue to grow spiritually in Christ. Our existence is not based on what we can do or acquire, but rather on the opportunities to impact the lives of others in our service to God because everyone is given the gift of hospitality (1 Peter 4:8-10). Therefore, *"who we really are"* is not defined by our reflection in a mirror, but by the reflection of Christ Who lives within us. The more we grow spiritually in Christ, the more we become who God created us to be.

God is Pleased. While learning to live a life that is pleasing to God (Micah 6:8; Hebrews 11:6), occasionally, we may wonder if God is pleased. We love God wholeheartedly, read and study the Bible—though not always as consistently as we should. We give tithes and offerings, pray and ask God for guidance, tell others about Christ, love and forgive others. Even still, there are times when we wonder if God is pleased because we know that we can never repay Him for all that He has done. It just may be worth it to check ourselves from time to time and make sure we are not going through the motions or a routine. God is worth more than a nonchalant response to His majesty.

As we desire to please God, we can rest assured that if we are not doing what God wants us to do He will definitely let us know. In the meantime, every now and then, take the time to be still (Psalm 46:10) and quiet your thoughts. It's not easy and you may find that you can't completely quiet your thoughts, but just try. At least rest your thoughts just for a little while and allow God to speak. Don't think of what you expect Him to say, just be quiet and be still. He may or may not say anything at the moment, but because you showed up to rest at His feet, even for just a little while, you are in His presence and He is pleased.

Wait . . . Don't Tell Me! No, really . . . don't tell me! How many times do you find yourself in the middle of a conversation about someone else? You didn't start it and you wish you didn't have to hear it. As soon as someone mentions something that has nothing to do with you and nothing to do with the person speaking, it's considered gossip. At that point, your task is to immediately change the subject. Never take part in gossip. Even if you are not adding any content to the conversation you are contributing just by giving the gossiper a platform to speak.

Til' We Get There (Heaven). For now, we can only image how wonderful it will be to finally see our Heavenly Father face to face. So how do we wait? How do we go about our everyday lives until the time comes? We use this time to be a reflection of God by the way we respond to others.

Although we sometimes respond to life and to others in a manner that is unpleasing to God, we can try to do better with each new opportunity. Our God is awesome. Who else would allow us to keep trying *til' we get there.*

Perfecting our Parenting. Children are full of surprises. We never know what will happen next. We watch them grow and we hope that they follow our instructions more than some of our examples because we are not perfect either.

Sometimes they listen, but many times they still go their own way. If we truly love them, we pray for them and chastise them with love when they need correction. No matter what we do for them, sometimes they have to learn by the consequences of their actions, just as we continue learning through our life experiences. In essence, while we wade through the channels of parenting, our goal is to focus on being the parent God called us to be (Ephesians 6:4; Psalm 127:3,4).

Every Day. I think I can actually say that every day is a good day! Not because everything happens just the way I want, but because everything that happens has a purpose for good (Romans 8:28). I will even go as far as to say that every day is a great day! Not because nothing unfavorable will happen, but because God created this day and God is Great! (Psalm 48:1; 86:10; 95:3; 145:3) So, every day is actually a good day, and yes, even a great day!

Nothing's Too Hard for God. God's response to our prayer requests does not define His capabilities. God has sole authority to decide whether or not to move on a situation according to His purpose. God can do anything because He created everything (Colossians 1:16; John 1:3; Romans 11:36). Therefore, nothing is too hard for God (Jeremiah 32:17).

"[14]And this is the confidence that we have in him, that, if we ask any thing according to his will, he heareth us: [15]And if we know that he heareth us, whatsoever we ask, we know that we have the petitions that we desired of him" (1 John 5:14, 15). Does this mean that we will receive everything we request? NO! The key component in this Scripture is that we must ask for what is *"according to God's will."* We can do so, if we are *living according*

to His will. Thus, He will honor our request because it is in His will. It may not happen when we expect, but God always keeps His promises (Hebrews 10:23; Zephaniah 3:5) in His time which is always perfect.

For Further Enrichment. Here are your instructions. Pick up your Bible, no matter how you are feeling. Before reading, pray for guidance, understanding, and wisdom. If you don't already have a personal Bible study plan, open the Bible and turn to the page wherever the Holy Spirit leads you. You can't go wrong because *"16All scripture is given by inspiration of God, and is profitable for doctrine, for reproof, for correction, for instruction in righteousness: 17That the man of God may be perfect, throughly furnished unto all good works"* (2 Timothy 3:16,17). Read what the Lord has led you to read. When you have finished, pray thanking God for His Words of encouragement and ask Him to help you retain what you have read.

Soon you will realize that reading the Word of God is like verbally speaking with our Heavenly Father one to One in a place far away from the distractions of life. It is a place where your spirit can relax in His presence while He empowers you with truth and light. At the end of this time well spent, you feel refreshed, new, and alive, like you've met the Lord for the first time. You feel safe and secure in the very Word that gives you hope, peace, joy, and the feeling of being loved like never before. WARNING: these feelings may only last for a while since a faithful relationship with the Lord is about loving Him enough to live by His Word and not about how His Word makes you feel. If reading God's Word only makes you feel better for the moment, then you may want to spend more time with the Lord by repeating these instructions as often as possible for further enrichment that leads to a lasting relationship.

The World Keeps Spinning. We can make progress in life if we follow God's plan rather than the expectations of the world. Influenced by many distractions, the world keeps spinning to fulfill its purpose regardless of whether or not it contributes to God's plan for our lives (Jeremiah 29:11). As far as we can see is not as far as we can go in life (Isaiah 55:9). By faith, we can accomplish what God has purposed (Hebrews 11:1)—that which is far greater than we realize. Whether or not we follow God's plan, His purpose will be fulfilled (Isaiah 55:10,11).

While the world keeps spinning, achieving no lasting results (1 John 2:17), those who abide by God's plan move forward to fulfill the will of God and receive the blessings He promised, *"For all the promises of God in him [Christ] are yea, and in him Amen, unto the glory of God by us"* (2 Corinthians 1:20). Therefore, all we need to do is take the first small step of faith (Luke 17:5,6), and keep our eyes on Christ to lead us the rest of the way (Hebrews 12:2). Living the life God intended allows us to move forward rather than aimlessly spinning in circles.

My Challenge For You. There are many familiar Scriptures in the Bible that we hear over and over during church sermons or other Bible-based gatherings. Well, my challenge to everyone is to find and read Scriptures that are less familiar in order to start seeing all the Scriptures from a fresh perspective. When we explore the entire Word of God we open our hearts to God's new mercies. *"[21] This I recall to my mind, therefore have I hope. [22] It is of the Lord's mercies that we are not consumed, because his compassions fail not. [23] They are new every morning: great is thy faithfulness".*

I selected the following Scripture because it is an encouraging reminder of the future dwelling place for believers in Christ. *"[1] His foundation is in the holy mountains. [2] The Lord loveth the gates of Zion more than all the dwellings of Jacob. [3] Glorious things are spoken of thee, O city of God. Selah [which means, now reflect on what you have just read]"* (Psalm 87:1-3).

The more we dive deeper into God's Word, the more we are encouraged, and the less likely the Scriptures will seem routine. Besides, strength and endurance comes from repetition. God's Word is a workout for the soul and refreshment for the spirit.

Comments | Blog Bites

Able to Stand

In Matthew 22:29, Jesus said we make a mistake by not knowing the Scriptures or the power of God. Studying the Bible is so much more than reading or memorizing Scriptures. Through application and the help of the Holy Spirit (2 Timothy 1:14), we come to know the principles of God's Word which allows us to experience the power of God. Chains of sin are broken, relationships are restored, and lives that were bound by hopelessness find new meaning.

Studying the Bible consistently prepares you for the uncertainties of life and allows you to be strong and withstand whatever may come against you. *"¹³Wherefore take unto you [put on] the whole armour of God, that ye may be able to withstand in the evil day, and having done all [overcome all], to stand. ¹⁴Stand therefore, having your loins girt about with truth, and having on the breastplate of righteousness; ¹⁵And your feet shod with the preparation of the gospel of peace; ¹⁶Above all, taking the shield of faith, wherewith ye shall be able to quench all the fiery darts of the wicked. ¹⁷And take the helmet of salvation, and the sword of the Spirit, which is the word of God:* (Ephesians 6:13-17).

Study and hold onto the Word in your mind and in your heart (Psalm 119:11). When you value and apply God's principles you begin to trust Him completely because He is the One and only true and living God, the Creator of Heaven and Earth, the One who will see us through every situation and circumstance. The Lord said, *"⁹ . . . I am God, and there is none else; I am God, and there is none like me. ¹⁰ . . . My counsel [purpose] shall stand, and I will do all my pleasure. ¹¹ . . . I have spoken it, I will also bring it to pass; I have purposed it, I will also do it [what I plan]* (Isaiah 46:9-10; 11). Trusting God allows us to keep His Word in the forefront of our minds and in the depths of our hearts so He will keep us from falling (Jude 1:24,25). His Word becomes our source of strength to overcome any situation.

Such powerful Words of assurance remind me that God will always fulfill His purpose in our lives when we commit to follow His will. He didn't say that our journey would be easy but He promised to guide us along the way. The Lord said *"Fear not: for I am with thee: . . ."* (Isaiah 43:5). Just know that whatever God allows you to go through, He has a plan. So be strong and don't be discouraged, no matter what. God never promised to prevent the unfavorable from happening, but He promised to strengthen and keep us (2 Thessalonians 3:3). Every person that we meet and every situation that we face plays a significant part in fulfilling the purpose God has planned.

While we grow spiritually we must never become intimidated by the enemy (Satan). Otherwise, we are demonstrating weakness through our lack of faith in Jesus Christ. We must remember that Christ already paid the price for our sin. Therefore we must walk in confidence because our Lord is Great. The Lord said, *"Ye are of God, little children, and have overcome them [every spirit that is not of God]: because greater is he that is in you, than he that is in the world"* (1 John 4:4). After years of tests and trials, I finally realized that I have to stand in total faith (Hebrews 11:1) to be able to stand at all, no matter the course. My observation over the years is that God wants us to see in ourselves what He sees in us because we are His children.

Through past experiences and studying the Word of God, I see every *"obstacle"* as another *"opportunity"* for God to reveal His *"omnipotence."* He knows our capabilities because our strength is in Him (Colossians 1:10,11). We are able to stand the tests of life when we are ready to accept the awesome work God is performing in and through us, for our good (Philippians 1:6) and for His glory (Isaiah 43:7).

Comments | Able to Stand

EPILOGUE

GOD IS OUR Heavenly Father, and as with all loving parents He wants to see His children move in the right direction. Yet, sometimes He allows us to go through unfavorable situations because they tend to provide the greatest opportunities for spiritual growth. Think of it this way, though we naturally enjoy a beautiful sunrise or sunset, we cannot forget the amazing sky after a storm.

With the guidance and protection of such a perfect Heavenly Parent we will live effectively (Psalm 60:12a) while we wait for Christ to return (1 Thessalonians 4:14-17). God already provided the perfect principles of living, available in the Holy Bible (2 Timothy 3:16). All we have to do is study and apply them. Why settle for a life torn by the deceptions of the enemy (Satan) and the condemnation of the world, when we can live in the liberty of our Savior Jesus Christ (Galatians 5:1).

Thank you for taking the time to read <u>BLESSINGS IN BLOGS: Living Effectively</u>. I hope that you will be encouraged by "Using the Upside of the Brain" to look up from your situations and focus on the One who can turn your burdens into blessings. With the effective use of this method, you will no longer yearn for glory days, but begin to live them.

"*15Blessed is the people that know the joyful sound: they shall walk, O Lord, in the light of thy countenance. 16In thy name shall they rejoice all the day: and in they righteousness shall they be exalted. 17For thou art the glory of their strength: and in thy favour our horn [power] shall be exalted. 18For the Lord is our defense; and the Holy One of Israel is our king*" (Psalm 89:15-18). When we keep our focus on the Lord and embrace the Living Word of God for strength, encouragement, and direction, we are blessed to live more effectively in Christ Jesus and glorify God in Heaven.

BLOGGING MY BACKGROUND

Learning to Walk

IF ASKED WHY I enjoy writing Christian content, I would say that the subject is intriguing, inspiring, and keeps me intimately linked to God's Word. Writing the blogs for this book required a great deal of Bible study that allowed me to reflect on the impact God has made in my life over the years as I came to know and love Jesus Christ.

When I was a child, I confessed Jesus Christ as my Lord and Savior and was baptized. Though I did not fully understand at the time the significance of what actually took place; over the years, with the spiritual guidance of the pastor, teachers, church family, and my family, I learned to love the Lord and depend on the Holy Spirit for direction. Yet, as an adult, until I finally came to know and understand the love of Christ (Ephesians 3:14-21), I still tried to live life my way (Luke 6:46-49). I did not realize that patiently waiting for God's response to my prayers is a part of spiritual growth, and that worrying (Luke 12:22-24) is basically criticizing His ability to handle my situations.

Basically, I learned that many of the difficult times I experienced over the years were the result of not allowing God to be in complete control of my life. In other words, I didn't fully trust Him. If I did, I would not have tried so hard to handle my life as I saw fit, and end up postponing the blessings God already planned for me. Nevertheless, as I continued growing spiritually, I rededicated my life to Christ and was baptized again with a better understanding of building a relationship with Him. Though Ephesians 4:5 says, *"One Lord, one faith, one baptism,"* because I was baptized as a child before I *fully* understood salvation, I chose to be baptized again as an adult to publically express the amazing change in my life.

Learning to trust the Lord is not an overnight achievement, but rather a process of learning to commit to God's way even though we may stumble occasionally. Like many Christians, I go through tough times that challenge my faith. Walking by faith is not easy because you don't know when and how your situation will turn out. If you knew, then your actions would be based on fact not faith (Hebrews 11:1). Through faith, you grow to trust the Lord more each day with each situation. You also grow by sharing your experiences with others, and reading about the experiences of the faithful individuals mentioned in the Bible (Hebrews Chapter 11).

After rededicating my life to Christ as an adult, I wanted to read the entire Bible but never took the time to do so. I made several attempts but kept starting over because I didn't understand the Bible that I had which was the King James Version. Then I decided to start reading the first four books of the New Testament: Matthew, Mark, Luke, and John, which provide an amazing account of the Gospel (the life and teachings of Jesus Christ). I am not suggesting that it is better to start with the New Testament. I just found that studying the life of Christ first was an effective way for me to come to know the Savior. In other words, how can you trust someone you don't know?

Once I committed to reading the Bible consistently, the scriptures were much easier to understand (Psalm 119:27) and I experienced greater peace while waiting for God's response. I also found that I learned something new with every personal study, even if it was something I read once before. *"For whatsoever things were written aforetime were written for our learning, that we through patience and comfort of the scriptures might have hope"* (Romans 15:4). What I have already read, I now see with a fresh perspective.

Before reading, I always pray that God will prepare my heart (James 5:16; Psalm 51:10) to receive what He is about to reveal through the Holy Spirit (2 Peter 1:20-21; Psalm 119:125). Prayer is how we speak to God.

Reading and hearing His Word is how God speaks to us. His Word is powerful. It teaches us how to discern right from wrong (Hebrews 4:12).

When I started spending more time with the Lord on a personal basis: praying with confidence in His direction, fasting in faith for more of Him, and reading my Bible regularly, I began to see Him as my best Friend (John 15:13-15; James 2:23). I also see Him as my Teacher (Matthew 4:23) who stays with me through every course. As this relationship continues to grow, I am able to find peace and strength to overcome any situation while I allow the Lord to lead me every step of the way. The more I read God's Word, the more I learn about life and what God is calling me to do.

I certainly do not claim to be an ordained minister or theological scholar. Up to the start of this blog, I had only read the Holy Bible in its entirety twice (the King James Version and the New International Version). To supplement my personal Bible study, I also connect with a local church for spiritual guidance and to participate in a collective worship of God. Coming together with other believers in Christ during worship services, Bible study classes, fellowships, and other faith-building opportunities is a beautiful way to honor God. He certainly deserves the special attention that we readily give each other when we gather for birthdays or other special occasions. A collective effort makes a great impact that demonstrates the love we have for our Lord. I believe that God is pleased when we take the time to step out of our comfort zone to come into His presence, rather than always expecting Him to come into ours.

While employed seven years as a church administrative assistant and secretary, I wrote articles for a newsletter that I designed, and fulfilled other office related duties. Serving in various ministries, I enjoyed singing with the choir and the praise team, and I also developed and coached a jump rope team to minister to youth through fitness, faith, and fun. To reach out to youth and adults, I organized a team of technical professionals to provide a computer lab for the community and technical support for church members and office staff. Currently, I write content for a ministry website that I developed and continue to maintain. Every opportunity God allowed taught me to humbly serve Him and others for His glory.

Years after receiving a Bachelor of Science in Business Administration in Marketing, God provided another educational opportunity which allowed me to pursue a Masters of Applied Science in Information and Communications Technology with a focus in Web Development and Design. This blessing will prepare me for publishing ministry content more effectively worldwide. I can't think of a more fulfilling way to bless God and others than to share the blessings I have received from God. I always try to keep in mind what the Apostle Paul wrote, "*2Set your affection [desire] on things above, not on things on the earth. 23And whatsoever ye do, do it heartily, as to the Lord, and not unto men; 24Knowing that of the Lord ye shall receive the reward of the inheritance: for ye serve the Lord Christ*" (Colossians 3:2, 23,24).

Certainly, following Christ as an example (John 13:15) is about more than serving in a ministry. It is about embracing the character of Christ to function in a way that is pleasing to God. Though being active in the things of God gives me the opportunity to utilize my God-given abilities, I never started learning to walk with Christ until I learned the significance of applying God's Word to every aspect of my life.

GUIDE TO PROPEL YOUR PURPOSE

ONE EVENING I was watching a new television program about a chaplain who served in a military medical facility struggling with her faith in God. Experiencing the devastating results of war, even *her* faith was shaken after seeing a deplorable number of wounded soldiers covered in blood, barely fighting for their lives. One soldier, realizing the extent of his injuries, asked for the chaplain to come and pray for him. Though dealing with a battle of her own, the chaplain went to him and promised to stay by his side as long as he needed. During the soldier's surgery, an overconfident lead surgeon made it clear to the chaplain that his faith was completely in himself and his abilities. He obviously didn't realize that he and his abilities belong to God (Galatians 3:26).

As I continued watching this program I was moved by the spiritual message that was unfolding. Though the surgery was successful, even with all the money the surgeon earned, he was incapable of healing his own brother who suffered from mental challenges. The surgeon's heart seemed so heavy with the war between loving his brother and knowing that there was nothing he could do to help; he finally realized that all he needed was Christ in his life. In the midst of his spiritual battle He came to know that God is *Greater* than his abilities, his money, and his fame. That is to say, God is Greater than some people ever care to admit. I believe that deep down inside, like everyone who chooses to reject God, the surgeon always knew that his life was nothing without God. He just didn't want to accept the reality of God's sovereignty.

This television episode reminded me that when people rebel against others, against life, or against themselves, they are lashing out against the love of Christ. They do this subconsciously because deep down inside they know right from wrong. Born in sin (Psalm 51:5), our spirit naturally wars between good and evil. Everyone at some point in their lives has an opportunity to choose to serve God or self. Self without God, is influenced by the enemy (Satan) who deceives and destroys, but is already defeated (Revelation 12:9).

Then I realized the fact that when people try so hard to convince themselves that they don't need God, their effort actually proves that God is Greater. We only fight what we see as a threat—something or someone who we believe has the power to stop us from doing what we want to do. Those who rebel against God choose to do so because they want to keep living life the way they think is easier, more satisfying, or limitless. They fail to realize that they are actually limiting themselves from being all that they were originally designed to be. Sooner or later, one way or another, they have to face the reality of God's sovereignty; either while they still have time on Earth, or at the feet of Jesus—the point at which it is too late (Isaiah 55:6; Matthew 24:29,30; Romans 14:11,12; Galatians 6:5; Romans 2:6).

What became of the chaplain? When the surgeon realized that he could not continue rejecting God, he went to see the chaplain for spiritual guidance. Such a small step of faith from the surgeon was the start of a new life for him and restoration of faith for the chaplain.

God wants us to love Him more than anything or anyone else because He is the Greatest Love we could ever behold (John 15:13; 1 John 4:8-12). He demonstrated His incredible love through the sacrificial Lamb of God—Jesus Christ, God's only begotten Son (John 1:14, John 3:16). By accepting Jesus Christ as our Lord and Savior we enter into a lasting relationship with Him—the most fulfilling relationship we will ever have throughout eternity.

Realizing that life in Jesus Christ is the only way to have the most productive and satisfying life on Earth, we become aware of our divine purpose. If we stay focused on God and continue following Christ—the Good Shepherd who leads His sheep, we will find greener pastures (Psalm 23). When we finally understand that our greatest achievements are by the grace and power of God, we will not allow anything or anyone that is not of the Spirit of God to get in the way. Even when we think that we are already extraordinary, there is something even greater that God can achieve in and through our lives (Ephesians 1:9-12; Jeremiah 29:11). *"Neither yield ye your members as instruments [weapons] of unrighteousness unto sin: but yield yourselves unto God, as those that are alive from the dead, and your members as instruments of righteousness unto God"* (Romans 6:13).

Are you ready to walk in the life you were originally designed to live? Maybe you are too busy trying to do what you think is right for you, or what others try to convince you to do. Maybe you are so distracted you cannot hear God calling you to your destiny. God's purpose for you is the only accomplishment that *satisfies* and *perfects* everything about you.

The following is a guide to help you start walking in God's purpose for your life. Be aware that once you start, the enemy (Satan) will try even harder to convince you otherwise (1 Peter 5:8). Do not allow the enemy to steal another second of your life while trying to handle things on your own. Turn everything over to God and the enemy will flee (James 4:7). Keep your focus and remember that through Christ, God has already equipped you for your destiny (1 Corinthians 2:12-16; 1 Corinthians 12:1-11). Just stay the course and you will reach the finish line. *"And let us not be weary in well-doing: for in due season we shall reap, if we faint not"* (Galatians 6:9). Here's how to endure:

1. Pray in faith, thanking God for the positive change that He is about to make in your life and ask Him for guidance to help you follow His will (Psalm 143:10).

2. Pray that God will reveal to you the purpose He has just for you. Make a list of the thing(s) you've always dreamed of accomplishing, not what would simply be great to do, but something that has tugged at your spirit for quite some time.

3. List the hindrances, the reason(s) you haven't started working towards this dream *(i.e., fear, doubt, or lack of any of the following: faith in God, confidence, employment, finances, skills, education, support from family and friend, etc.).*

4. Of these hindrances, has your circumstances changed in any way that would now allow you to move forward?
   If yes, skip to the *Thoughts of Encouragement.*

5. If your circumstances haven't changed, then consider how God can change *your outlook about yourself and about others* through the help of the Holy Spirit. Then take a look at the following thoughts of encouragement provided to help clear the clouds of doubt and frustration, and renew your mind and spirit to function more effectively in Christ (Also, refer to the technique "Using the Upside of the Brain" (June 1 of the Summer Section).

THOUGHTS OF ENCOURAGEMENT

- **Know who you are.**
  A child of God (John 1:12)
  A friend of God (John 15:14)
  Chosen by God (1 Peter 2:9)
  Redeemed and forgiven (Colossians 1:14)
  Chosen to bear fruit (John 15:16)

- **Know how much God loves you.**
  God loves you dearly (John 3:16)
  God loved you before you loved Him (1 John 4:10)
  No one loves you more than God (John 15:13)

God loves to give to His children (John 14:13,14;
1 John 3:22)
Nothing shall separate you from God's love
(Romans 8:38,39)

- **Know your true purpose.**
  God has given each of us specific abilities (Acts 11:29;
  Ephesians 4:11,12)
  God wants us to prosper (Jeremiah 29:11)
  We are blessed to do God's will (Ephesians 1:3-6)
  God provides instruction so we can succeed (Psalm
  32:8; 2 Timothy 3:16,17)
  Everything will work out according to His purpose
  (Romans 8:28)

- **Know the power that is within you.**
  The Holy Spirit of God dwells within you to lead you
  (1 John 3:23,24; Romans 8:14)
  Greater is He that is within you than he that is in the
  world (1 John 4:1-4)
  If God is for you, who can stand against you
  (Romans 8:31)
  You are more than a conqueror through Christ
  (Romans 8:36-37)

- **Know that loving yourself allows you to love God and
  others.**
  Your love for others should reflect the love you have
  for yourself (Leviticus 19:18; Matthew 19:19; Matthew
  22:37-39; Mark 12:29-31; Luke 10:27; Romans 13:9;
  Galatians 5:14)
  You will do well if you love others as you love yourself
  (James 2:8)

You should never hate yourself (Ephesians 5:29)
God will give you some of the desires of your heart
when you follow His will (Psalm 37:4)

- **Review the Thoughts of Encouragement** as often as it takes to stay encouraged.

6. Pray about the following: (1) that God will help you use His resources wisely (Psalm 119:133) to fulfill His purpose in your life, and (2) that He will give you the courage and strength (Psalm 29:11) to maintain your focus on His plan without giving in to distractions, worry, doubt, or fear, no matter what.

7. List the individuals that have been very supportive in your positive endeavors (*These are the people with whom you can share your plans to keep you encouraged*).

8. List the individuals that have been critical of your positive endeavors (*These are the people you shouldn't expect to support you in your plans; but they may actually keep you determined to follow through. It's all in how you choose to perceive them*).

9. Expect to succeed no matter what happens or how long it takes. Remember, *there is nothing too hard for God* (Genesis 18:13,14; Jeremiah 32:17). *With God all things are possible* (Matthew 19:26; John 15:5).

10. *Trust God* (Proverbs 3:5,6), step out on faith (Matthew 14:22-33), and be ready for God to reveal His plan (Psalm 143:8).

11. Be patient and wait on God because, *"The Lord is good unto them that wait for him, to the soul that seeketh him"* (Lamentations 3:25).

12. Log your progress, including any obstacles and achievements. Then you will always be aware and grateful for all that God is doing in and through your life.

DEFINITIONS

Book References:

[1]**Discernment:** ability to distinguish or perceive differences.

[2]**Edify:** morally or spiritually educate, improve, strengthen or uplift.

[3]**Humanity:** the human species, mankind, the human race, (men and women).

[4]**Sanctify:** set apart for sacred use to make holy.

[5]**Saved:** those who believe that Jesus Christ is the Son of God and accept Him as their Lord and Savior.

[6]**Talent:** (Hebrew/Greek) a Biblical measure worth approximately 3000 shekels, 60 minas, or 75/88 U.S. pounds. Various translations refer to talent(s) as 1000 pounds (Holman Bible Publishers, 1991, p. 1404)

[7]**Unsaved:** those who do not believe or have faith in God.

References for General Bible Study (KJV):

Atonement: reconciliation (numbers 28:22)

Bear *(his sin):* be responsible for (Leviticus 24:15)

Blasphemy: act as if God doesn't exist (Leviticus 24:10-16); spoken against (2 Kings 19:3; Luke 12:10)

Consecrate: undergo purification rites as a reminder of one's sinfulness and God's holiness (Joshua 3:5; 7:13)

Covenant: agreement (Leviticus 24:8)

Dispensation: allowance, exemption, plan (Ephesian 1:10)

Establish: make strong (Proverbs 24:3)

Fear God: respect, reverence God (Leviticus 19:3)

Flesh: mortal lives, carnal (2 Corinthians 4:11)

Froward: perverse (Deuteronomy 32:20); Proverbs 6:14)

Grace: unmerited favor (Romans 5:1-2; Galatians 5:4)

Hallowed: holy (Leviticus 19:8)

Justification: remedy for sin, process by which an individual is brought into an unmerited, right relationship with God (Genesis 12:1-3)

Manifest: obvious, evident, visible (2 Corinthians 4:11)

Mercy: compassion (Psalm 103:8)

Perfecting: equipping (Ephesians 4:12)

Principalities: prestige (Jeremiah 13:18)

Quicken: revive (Psalm 119:37)

Rebuke: disagreement (Proverbs 27:5)

Redeem: to buy back (Leviticus 25:48; 26:15)

Remission: forgiveness (Hebrews 10:18)

Repent: ask God for forgiveness and abandon your sin

Reproach: belittle (Psalm 74:22)

Reproach: disgrace (Proverbs 14:34)

Reprobate: rejected, unfit (Romans 1:28)

Sanctify: set apart (Hebrews 10:10)

Stiffnecked people: rebellious (Exodus 33:3)

Terrible: to be respected (Psalm 47:2)

Trespass: guilt (Leviticus 19:21)

Uncircumcised: unfit (Leviticus 19:23)

Waxen: become (Deuteronomy 31:20)

SCRIPTURE INDEX

Scriptures and keywords or phrases referenced in each blog by section.

SUMMER SECTION

June 1—Using the Upside of the Brain

The peace that God promised (John 14:27)

Works of the flesh (Galatians 5:17)

Grow in grace and knowledge of the Lord (2 Peter 3:18)

Trust in the Lord (Proverbs 3:5)

There is nothing too hard for God (Jeremiah 32:17, 18b)

Refocus on Christ (Isaiah 26:3)

Remember God's Word (Psalm 119:11)

Renew your mind (Romans 12:2)

Praise the Lord (Psalm 86:12)

We are confident in Christ (1 John 5:14)

For all have sinned and come short of the glory of God (Romans 3:23)

Christ's Deity (John 17:5)

Jesus' purpose (John 20:21; John 10:10)

We are perfected through Christ (1 Peter 5:10; Hebrews 10:14; Hebrews 12:23; Matthew 5:48)

Behold, all things are become new (II Corinthians 5:17)

Jesus the Messiah, fully man yet fully God (Philippians 2:5-8)

Walk in the will of God (Philippians 2:13)

In all things may God be glorified (1 Peter 4:11)

We can't possibly image all that God has prepared for them that love him (1 Corinthians 2:9)

Peace beyond all understanding (Philippians 4:7)

The basis of "Using the Upside of the Brain" (Ephesians 3:11-21)

God promised to never leave or forsake me (Hebrews 13:5b)

I can do all things through Christ (Philippians 4:13)

In all things I am more than a conqueror through Christ Jesus (Romans 8:37)

All things work together for good (Romans 8:28)

God's Word will not go out and come back void (Isaiah 55:11)

June 3—Never a Dull Moment

Rest from our heavy burdens (Matthew 11:28-30)

From God's perspective (Psalm 113:5,6)

The trials of life are expected (1 Peter 4:12,13)

Though we have tribulation, Christ overcame the world (John 16:33)

June 7—The Greatest Investment

Set your affection on things above, not on things on the Earth (Colossians 3:2)

Where your treasure is (Matthew 6:19-21)

Salvation is a gift from God through Christ Jesus (Romans 6:23)

God wants everyone to be saved (1 Timothy 2:3,4)

June 18—I Believe That Was Yesterday

We must forgive (Colossians 3:12,13)

The Lord forgives (Matthew 6:14)

Sin separates us from God (Isaiah 59:2)

We are saved by grace (Ephesians 2:8)

Power and authority is God's (Matthew 28:18)

God will repay those who do evil against you (Romans 12:19)

God's love is unconditional (Romans 5:8;Romans 8:38,39)

Everyone falls short of God's glory (Romans 3:23)

Tomorrow is not promised (Proverbs 27:1; Romans 13:10,11)

Whatever is holding you captive let it go (Philippians 3:13,14)

June 24—What Did You Learn?

Children of God (Galatians 3:26)

Adversity stimulates communication with God (Jonah 2:1,2)

The Lord will teach us to do His will (Psalm 143:10)

July 4—Live Like We Are Saved

We are saved by the blood that Jesus Christ (Matthew 27:33; Mark 15:22)

Christ died for our sins on Calvary (Luke 23:33)

The purpose (Ephesians 1:7)

Gift of a brand new life (2 Corinthians 5:17)

God desires all to be saved (1 Timothy 2:4,5)

With the mouth confession is made unto salvation (Romans 10:9,10;
     Acts 16:31)

Only Christ could pay such a debt because He is sinless
     (2 Corinthians 5:21)

Eternal death (Matthew 25:41,46; 2 Thessalonians 1:9)

There is no other Savior (Isaiah 43:11)

Christ is the only way to our Heavenly Father (John 14:6)

We are forgiven (1 John 1:9)

We are accepted through Christ (2 Corinthians 5:9)

Our love for others should be a reflection of our love for Christ
     (1 John 4:17,20)

The wages of sin is death; the gift of God is eternal life through
     Christ (Romans 6:23)

We don't have to carry the weight of sin (Hebrews 12:1,2)

We are covered by the blood of Jesus Christ (Romans 5:6-9)

Think good thoughts (Philippians 4:8)

We are blessed when we follow Christ (Deuteronomy 7:11-14)

Disobedience leads to struggles we could otherwise avoid
     (Jonah Chapter 1)

The love God has shown (John 3:16)

July 13—Point of Reference

God will lead you (Psalm 27:11)

Everyone has gone astray from time to time (Isaiah 53:6)

Repent and turn from sin (Mark 6:12; Hosea 14; Isaiah 55:6,7)

The Lord will cleanse us from all unrighteousness (1 John 1:9)

Christ paid the price once and for all (1 Peter 3:18)

We are recipients of God's grace (Ephesians 2:8,9)

We are forgiven if we humble ourselves, pray, seek God, and repent
(2 Chronicles 7:14)

July 24—Walk It Out

God never changes (James 1:17)

God has a plan for your life (Jeremiah 29:11)

Keep God first and He will bless you with some of the desires of your hear
(Psalm 37:4)

August 5—What Was That All About?

Praise God in the congregation of the people (Psalm 107:32)

Trouble is forever present (Deuteronomy 4:30,31; 1 Peter 4:12-13; Romans
5:3; Ephesians 3:13,14; 1 Peter 1:7; Acts 9:15,16; 2 Corinthians 1:3-7;
John 16:33)

God tests our faith (Proverbs 17:3)

Through faith we have peace (Romans 5:1)

God's thoughts and ways are higher than what we could ever think or do
(Isaiah 55:8-9)

No one knows everything about God (Romans 11:34, ASV)

God is the Creator (Romans 11:36)

The Lord never fails (Zephaniah 3:5)

God is our help and strength (Psalm 46:1)

Be still, and know that God is the Almighty (Psalm 46:10)

August 19—Spiritual Ailments Part 1: Defined

Obedience to God's Word sustains our physical health (Proverbs 4:20-22)

God wants everyone to be saved (1 Timothy 2:3,4)

Sin separates us from God (Isaiah 59:2)

Human tendency to sin (Isaiah 64:6)

Sin separates us from God (Isaiah 59:2)

Through Christ we have peace because He overcame the world of
tribulations (John 16:33)

Trust God's promises beyond your understanding (Numbers 23:19;
Romans 3:4; Proverbs 3:5,6)

The power of God will be made known (John 9:1-7)

God cares (Psalm 55:22, and 1 Peter 5:7)

Conceited pride is self-destructive (1 Timothy 3:6; Proverbs 16:18,19;)

The cause of Satan's downfall (Isaiah 14:12-20; Luke 10:18-19; 2 Peter 1:19)

God's grace is sufficient to develop us (2 Corinthians 12:9)

August 31—Spiritual Ailments Part 2: Healing

Seek the kingdom of God and His righteousness first (Matthew 6:33)

We all follow our own way from time to time (Isaiah 53:6)

Stay focused on God (Hebrews 12:2)

Pray continuously (1 Thessalonians 5:17)

Stay with Christ and He will stay with you (John 15:4)

Be faithful and make an honest effort to carry out God's plan
(1 Corinthians 4:2; Matthew 25:21)

We are sanctified[5] by the Lord's Word of Truth (John 17:17)

Prayer is essential (Hebrews 11:6)

God is our Heavenly Father (2 Corinthians 6:17,18)

"Blessed are the pure in heart: for they shall see God" (Matthew 5:8)

Intercessory prayer helps others (Job 16:21; Genesis 18:16-33)

Praise God with our voice (Hebrews 13:15)

God knows us completely (Psalm 139:1,2)

Faith keeps us afloat (Matthew 14:27-31)

Through Christ we can escape any temptation (1 Corinthians 10:13)

The wages of sin is death (Romans 6:23)

FALL SECTION

September 1—What's My Motivation?

    Seek the kingdom of God and His righteousness first (Matthew 6:33)

    I survive because Christ is within me (Galatians 2:20)

    God is not a physical being; He is a Spirit (John 4:24)

    God is love (1 John 4:8)

    Praise God for all His wondrous works (Psalm 107:8, 15, 21, and 31)

    God provides daily (Matthew 6:11)

    God's compassionate desire is that all will be saved (Matthew 18:11-14;
        1 Timothy 2:1-4)

    God is ALL (Exodus 3:14; Matthew 22:32; 1 John 4:8; John 4:24; Colossians
        1:15-17; Psalm 47; Psalm 146:5-10; Exodus 32:9-14; Isaiah 9:6; John
        14:6-10; John 5:22-23)

    God is a rewarder of those who diligently seek Him (Hebrews 11:6b)

    Seek God's face (2 Chronicles 7:14) not His hand.

    God supplies all that we need (Philippians 4:19)

    God demonstrated the extent of His desire to bless us (Romans 8:32)

    Give thanks to God for all He has done (1 Thessalonians 5:18)

September 10—Forever in my Heart

    For those in Christ, beyond this life we are in the presence of the Lord
        (2 Corinthians 5:8)

    We will receive a heavenly body (1 Corinthians 15:49-52)

    We will all face judgment according to what we have done
        (2 Corinthians 5:10)

    Christ is the bread of life (John 6:58)

    Our resurrected body will be like Christ's glorified body
        (Philippians 3:20, 21)

    Christ is the doorway to God (John 10:7-9)

    Through Christ we have everlasting life (John 11:25,26;
        John 3:16; Hebrews 5:9)

    There is so much more to life with God (Luke 23:43)

Life on Earth is temporary (Matthew 6:19)

Our heavenly reward is based on the life we live (1 Corinthians 3:8; Revelations 22:12)

Live to fulfill your purpose (John 17:4; Matthew 25:21)

We all belong to God (John 17:9,10)

God allows us to choose whether or not to serve Him (Joshua 24:15)

September 29—Reinforcing the Seems

Through Christ we can do all things (Philippians 4:13)

The Lord will work out whatever is binding your spiritual growth (Philippians 2:12-13)

God knows us better than we know ourselves (Matthew 10:3)

Use your gifts from God wisely (Matthew 25:14-30)

God will help you complete what He allowed you to begin (Philippians 1:6; James 1:12)

God will never leave you comfortless (John 14:18)

Be committed; a double-minded person is unstable (James 1:8)

The trials we face are necessary so that our joy in the Lord will be complete (John 15:1-11)

Christ is the Son of the only TRUE and LIVING GOD (Psalm 18:46)

The Lord is great clothed honor and majesty (Psalm 104:1)

The Lord's grace is sufficient (2 Corinthians 12:9)

The Lord's mercy endures forever (Psalm 136:2)

God's love is unconditional (I Corinthians 13)

God's love never fails (1 Corinthians 13:8; Psalm 136)

God is Love (1 John 4:8 and 16)

God allows us to have a personal relationship with Him (Exodus 33:11-23)

God loves us so much (John 3:16)

Faith defined (Hebrews 11:1)

Trust the Lord beyond your understanding and He will direct your paths (Proverbs 3:5)

October 11—Think On These Things

Don't dwell on the past (Isaiah 43:18)

Maintain good thoughts (Philippians 4:8-9)

October 14—Share Your Faith

Spread the Gospel of Jesus Christ (Matthew 28:19-20; Luke 24:47;
     Philippians 1:27; 2 Timothy 2:1-2)

Be a witness (Isaiah 43:9-11)

We are light in this world so others will come to know Christ (Romans 2:19)

There is no need to worry about how to speak for Christ (Matthew 10:19, 20)

We are God's instruments of righteousness (Romans 6:12, 13)

We are the salt of the Earth (Matthew 5:13)

All have sinned (Romans 3:23)

We should not judge others without first judging ourselves (Matthew 7:1-5)

Jesus is the Light of the world (John 8:12)

The Most High God (Genesis 14:20)

Encourage others to be saved (1 Corinthians 10:32-33)

God desires to have all of His children with Him (1 Timothy 2:1-6)

The Great Commission (Matthew 28:18-20)

Jesus Christ, was fully God and fully man (John 14:7)

Sometime after His resurrection and after being seen by several (1
     Corinthians 15:1-8), before He

Christ ascended to Heaven and sat at the right hand of the Father
     (Mark 16:19)

Christ promised to return for us (2 Peter 3:1-10)

Spirit of Truth (the Comforter) (John 14:16-17)

As we go through the trials of life (John 16:33)

God, Jesus Christ, and the Holy Spirit are One (Matthew 28:19-20)

Three persons of the Godhead (Colossians 2:9; Matthew 28:19b)

Christ gave His life so that we may have everlasting life (John 3:16) with the

The One and Only, True and Living God (1 Thessalonians 1:9)

Jesus Christ is the only Way to receive salvation (John 14:6)

God has a plan for each of our lives (Jeremiah 29:11)

free from condemnation (Romans 8:1)

A brand new life in Christ (2 Corinthians 6:17)

There is no greater love than the love of Christ (John 15:13)

How you can to start a relationship with Christ (Romans 10:9-10)

You can accomplish all things through Christ who gives you strength
(Philippians 4:13)

October 30—Now and Forever

Lord gives them light who will serve Him eternally (Revelation 22:3-5)

We will praise God forever (Psalm 34:1; Psalm 150:1).

We will worship the Lord continuously throughout eternity
(Revelation 4:8)

We are save by grace not works else we would boast (Ephesians 2:8-9)

The faithful will receive a reward (Revelation 22:12; Isaiah 40:10)

The Word of God shall stand forever (Isaiah 40:8)

November 1—From Point A to Point B

We are called by God to be a light to others (Isaiah 42:6)

Seven is the Biblical number of completion (Genesis 8:4)

God is in control (Proverbs 20:24)

We can find direction in God's Word (Psalm 119:105)

Man's natural will (Romans 7:15)

We must stay on course and not turn to the left or right (Proverbs 4:27)

November 4—The Absolute Fulfillment of Life

Moving forward to fulfill my calling (Philippians 3:14)

I can do all things through Christ who gives me strength (Philippians 4:13)

Serving others is essential to further God's kingdom (Galatians 6:10;
Romans 12:10-13)

Support the development of the church (1 Corinthians 12:4-14;27-31)

God rested (Genesis 2:3)

God is our Creator (Ephesians 3:9)

Keep God above all that you aspire to achieve so not to squander the
blessings He has given (Luke 15:11-16)

Life is more than our possessions (Luke 12:15)

Believers can enjoy the fruits of their service in the Lord (Psalm 128:1,2)

Seek the kingdom of God first (Matthew 6:31-33)

God will supply all that we need (Philippians 4:19)

November 8—Today

God Created Heaven and Earth (Genesis 1:1)

Rejoice, for this is the day the Lord has made (Psalm 118:24)

God is always present (Matthew 28:20)

November 13—Be a Light

Stand firm in faith (1 Corinthians 16:13)

Let your light shine to glorify God (Matthew 5:14-16)

Jesus is the Light of the world (John 9:5)

God works in and through us to be effective for His kingdom
(Philippians 2:13-16)

The Word of God is powerful and a discerner of the thoughts and intents
of the heart (Hebrews 4:12)

We are ambassadors for Christ (2 Corinthians 5:20-21)

Christ was committed to fulfill the will of God (John 9:4)

Christ came not to condemn but to save the lost (John 3:17)

God is not pleased when we think too highly of ourselves (Romans 12:3)

He doesn't want us to take on the seductive character of pride
(Proverbs 8:13)

We must not conform to this world (Romans 12:2)

We are no longer bound by our old ways; we are made new through Christ
(2 Corinthians 5:17)

November 25—The Remedy

Genesis 7:12, 13, 15; 22:29

2 Samuel 22:50

I Chronicles 16:8, 24, 27, 35, 41; 25:3; 31:2

Ezra 3:11

Nehemiah 11:17; 12:8, 24, 27, 31, 38, 40, 46

Psalms 6:5; 18:49; 26:7; 30:4, 12; 35:18; 50:14; 69:30; 75:1; 79:13; 92:1; 95:2; 97:12; 100:4; 105:1; 106:1, 47; 107:1, 22; 116:17; 118:1, 29; 199:62; 122:4; 136:1, 2, 3, 26; 140:13; 147:7

Isaiah 51:3

Jeremiah 30:19

Daniel 6:10

Amos 4:5

Jonah 2:9

Matthew 15:36; 26:27

Mark 8:6; 14:23

Luke 2:38; 17:16; 22:17, 19

John 6:11, 23

Acts 27:35

Romans 14:6; 16:4

1 Corinthians 10:30; 11:24; 14:16, 17; 15:57

2 Corinthians 1:11; 2:14; 4:15; 8:16; 9:11, 12; 9:15

Ephesians 1:16; 5:4, 20

Philippians 4:6

Colossians 1:3, 12; 2:7; 3:17; 4:2

1 Thessalonians 1:2; 3:9; 5:18

2 Thessalonians 2:13

1 Timothy 2:1; 4:3, 4

Philemon 13:15

1 Peter 2:19

Revelation 4:9, 11; 7:12; 11:17

WINTER SECTION

December 8—The Opportunity No One Wants, But Everyone Needs
>With victory over death, Christ has overcome the world (John 16:33)
>Our strength is renewed when we wait on God (Isaiah 40:31)
>God will not fail or forsake us (Deuteronomy 31:6; Hebrews 13:5)
>Peace beyond comprehension (Philippians 4:7; Proverbs 3:5,6)
>We are strong even in the midst of uncertainties (2 Corinthians 12:10)

December 9—Growing Closer to God
>Nothing is too difficult for God (Genesis 18:14)
>With God all things are possible (Matthew 19:26; Luke 1:37)
>The Lord will comfort you (2 Corinthians 1:3)
>Tithing (Hebrews 7:4-9)
>God created all things as He pleased (Revelation 4:11)
>Everything works out for good, for those who are called according to God's purpose (Romans 8:28)
>We are the children of God (John 1:12; 1 John 3:1,2)
>Trust the Lord beyond your understanding and He will direct your paths (Proverbs 3:5,6)
>The Lord comforts you; then you can comfort others (2 Corinthians 1:4)

December 16—What Really Matters
>Do deeds in the name of the Lord (Colossians 3:17)
>Forgive (Ephesians 4:32; Colossians 3:13)
>No matter what, treat others as we would like to be treated (Luke 6:31)
>Bless the Lord (Psalm 34:1)
>Do for others as you would have other do for you (Matthew 7:12)
>The Lord is Greater above all else in this world (1 John 4:4b)

December 23—Choices
>God created us and knows us personally (Psalm 139:1-4)
>The Lord will guide us even in the midst of trouble (Psalm 138:7)

We can repent (Matthew 4:17)

Return to our Father (Luke 15:11-32).

Refrain from pride (Proverbs 16:18; James 4:6)

Everything works out for good, for those who are called
according to God's purpose (Romans 8:28)

Seek the Lord for guidance (Psalm 25:9)

New in Christ (2 Corinthians 5:17)

Jesus is the Light of the world (John 9:5)

Christ is ready to come into your heart if you allow Him (Revelation 3:20)

Christ wants us to have an abundant life (John 10:10)

We have eternal life through Christ (John 6:27; John 4:14)

To enter the kingdom of God, we must be born again by accepting
His gift of salvation (John 3:3;)

Rebirth is of water and spirit, not of flesh (John 3:5,6)

When we are born again, we become children of God (Romans 8:16,17;
Mark 10:15)

Grow in grace, and in the knowledge of our Lord (2 Peter 3:18)

Everyone is a sinner before receiving Christ (Psalm 51:5;
Romans 3:23; Isaiah 53:6)

Jesus Christ is the Son of God (Mark 1:11; 2 Peter 1:17,18; Matthew 27:43)

Christ is the only way for us to come into a right relationship with
God our Heavenly Father (John 14:6)

Only Christ can forgive our sins (Mark 2:7-12)

We are saved through the sacrificial blood of Jesus Christ when
He was crucified (Matthew 27:11-66)

When we verbally confess the Lord Jesus Christ, and believe in our hearts
that He died on the cross, was buried, and rose from the dead on
the third day, we are saved (Romans 10:9,10; 1 Corinthians 15:1-4;
Luke 24:46,47)

Full immersion by water baptism identifies us with the death, burial, and
resurrection of Christ (Romans 6:3,4)

We are a new creation in Christ (2 Corinthians 5:17)

Repent and be baptized (Acts 2:38)

We are free from sin to serve righteousness (Romans 6:18)

The love of Jesus Christ brings us into a relationship with God the Father,
God the Son, and God the Holy Spirit. Therefore, be confident in knowing
that you have eternal life through Jesus Christ (1 John 5:7, 11-13).

Serve the Lord with gladness (Psalm 100:2a)

Be an example of the believers in all your ways (1 Timothy 4:12)

Choose whom you will serve (Joshua 24:15)

Choose Christ today before it's too late (Matthew 24:42)

What will take place when Christ returns (Matthew 25:31-34)

December 25—Everlasting Peace and Incredible Joy

The birth of Christ (Luke 2:8-14; 21)

Christ is perfect (Matthew 5:48)

Christ is the only example of perfection (1 Timothy 1:16)

Because He created us, God knew us before our physical birth
(Jeremiah 1:5)

We can run our race in life if we stay focused on Christ (Hebrews 12:1-2)

January 1—God's Word in Prayer: Divine Intervention

The Spirit of the Father speaks in (Matthew 10:19-20) and through us
(Exodus 4:10-12)

"Blessed are the pure in heart: for they shall see God" (Matthew 5:8)

God gives us His undivided attention whenever we call on Him
(Psalm 65:2)

January 5—God's Word in Prayer: Scriptures, Pt. 1

The heart reveals the character of an individual (Luke 6:45)

David's prayer of adoration to God (1 Chronicles 29:10-13)

We must worship God in spirit and truth (John 4:24)

God already knows what we need (Matthew 6:8b)

The Lord's Prayer (The Model Prayer) (Matthew 6:9-13; Luke 11:2-4)

God cares (1 Peter 5:7)

God provides (Matthew 6:26)

All have sinned (Romans 3:23)

God forgives (Isaiah 43:25)

God will cleanse us of all unrighteousness (I John 1:9)

We are forgiven through the bloodshed of Christ (Hebrews 9:22)

Christ's sacrifice makes us right with God once and for all (1 Peter 3:18a)

We are redeemed through the blood of Christ (Ephesians 1:7)

Be kind and compassionate to others (Ephesians 4:32)

Forgive others and God will forgive you (Matthew 6:14,15)

The Lord will never leave or forsake us (Hebrews 13:5b)

Unfavorable times are certain on Earth as we look forward to eternal life
with our Lord (2 Corinthians 4:8-11,17)

We are more than conquerors and nothing shall separate us from the love
of Christ (Romans 8:37-39)

The Holy Spirit (The Comforter) will abide with us forever (John 14:16)

Strengthen one another (Romans 15:1,2)

God is love (1 John 4:8)

God loves us so much that He sacrificed His only begotten Son (John 3:16)

January 9—God's Word in Prayer: Scriptures, Pt. 2

Jesus prayed in the Garden of Gethsemane (Luke 22:39-44)

Trust the Lord beyond your understanding and He will direct your paths
(Proverbs 3:5-6)

Don't worry, praise and thank God and be at peace (Philippians 4:6-7)

Don't pray for other's approval (Matthew 6:5)

Don't be afraid, just believe (Mark 5:36b)

If you struggle with believing ask God to help your unbelief (Mark 9:24b)

God's Word in prayer encourages spiritual growth (Ephesians 3:14-21)

The Lord will lift us up if we wait on Him and don't give up
(Isaiah 40:28-31)

You will make it through your season of uncertainty if you do not give up
(Galatians 6:9)

Continue to pray always (1 Thessalonians 5:17)

Believe in faith that God will answer your prayer (Ephesians 6:18)

Make prayer a part of your daily regimen (Psalm 55:17)

January 10—A Spirit of Humility

Serve the Lord for the Lord and not to please others (Ephesians 6:6,7)

Don't worry about the opinion of others; do all to the glory of God (Colossians 3:23)

Know that you are blessed as you bless God (Ephesians 6:8)

Strengthen each other's weaknesses and benefit from each other's strengths (Proverbs 27:17)

January 11—People, Read Your Bible!

By His Spirit God reveals to the believers in Christ all that we need to know about His plan (1 Corinthians 2:13)

The deep things of God (1 Corinthians 2:10)

God reveals what He wants us to know (1 Corinthians 2:12)

The Word of God is able to judge our thoughts and intentions (Hebrews 4:12)

Support our families (1 Timothy 5:8)

Feed the hungry (Matthew 25:37)

Provide for the poor and homeless (Matthew 25:38)

Honor and care for the veterans (John 15:13) and the elderly (Leviticus 19:32; Psalm 71:9)

Committing crimes motivated by lust (2 Samuel 11:1-18)

Instigating or gossiping was as spiritually and concretely unproductive then as it is today (Ezra 4:6-24)

Judging other people's sin and shame continues these days (John 8:1-11)

Accusing the innocent continues these days (John 18:1-12)

Committing crimes of passion continues these days (2 Samuel 11:1-18)

Jesus Christ is the same yesterday, and today, and forever (Hebrews 13:8)

People may use profanity out of fear or denial (Matthew 26:74)

What seems right by man [an individual] (Proverbs 14:12; 16:25)

What is right by God (Psalm 1:1-4; 37:4)

However, that which is *against God* (Psalm 51:4) will always be sin.

We are free from the *condemnation of sin* (Romans 8:1)

The result of sin is death (Romans 6:23), prior to the blood of Christ

Profanity is unrighteous (Romans 3:9-14)

The blasphemous us of God and Jesus Christ (Leviticus 18:21b)

The use of profanity out of fear or denial (Matthew 26:74)

The use of wholesome words brings forth life (Proverbs 15:4)

Speak only what is acceptable to God (Psalm 19:14)

God calls homosexuality is an abomination [sin] (Leviticus 18:22)

New Testament reference to homosexuality (Romans 1:26, 27; 1 Timothy 1:8-11)

Humanity is no longer under the law (Romans 6:14)

How the Lord referred to eating certain foods as abomination [unfit]
(Leviticus Chapter 11)

All food is acceptable as long as it is received with thanksgiving, sanctified4
(set apart) by the Word of God and prayer (1 Timothy 4:3-5)

Consequence of immoral behavior (1 Corinthians 6:9-10)

God created woman as the only suitable partner for man (Genesis 2:18-22)

We are all born in sin (Psalm 51:5)

We are saved by the grace of God (Ephesians 2:8)

Jesus is the only way to the Father (John 14:6)

There is nothing new (Ecclesiastes 1:9)

God allows certain events so that His work will be made evident (John
9:3b; Genesis 22; Daniel Chapter 6; Mark 2:13-17; Luke Chapter 23)

Seek the Lord while He may be found (Isaiah 55:6)

January 25—Sisters

There is a season, and a time to every purpose (Ecclesiastes 3:1)

". . . fearfully and wonderfully made" by God (Psalm 139:14).

Real love is unconditional, not selfish, not easily provoked, or offended
(1 Corinthians 13)

What is united by God will not be divided (Mark 10:9)

February 5—Saved for a Purpose

Like sheep we all tend to go our own way from time to time (Isaiah 53:6)

We can call on the Lord to save us (Psalms 34:17;142:5-7; Romans 10:13)

Unlike humanity[3], God cares deeply for our soul (Psalm 142:4)

God hears us and will lift us up from our distress with his hand of
righteousness (Psalm 40:1,2; Isaiah 41:9,10)

His work is made evident unto man (Isaiah 41:20)

God will bring us out of darkness into His marvelous light (1 Peter 2:9)

Tell others about the good news of Jesus Christ (Matthew 28:19,20; Mark
16:15,16; Luke 24:46-48)

February 14—God's Love Is Forever

God's love is forever (Jeremiah 31:3)

God deeply loves us (Isaiah 43:3,4)

God wrote His master plan well before our time (Jeremiah 1:5)

Jesus sacrificed His life for us on the cross (Luke 19:10;
1 Corinthians 15:1-4)

We must put away our old corruptible ways to be renewed in the spirit
(Ephesians 4:22-25)

Do what is right and good according to the Lord (Deuteronomy 6:18)

If we confess our sins the Lord is faithful and just to cleanse us (1 John 1:9)

God is with us through thick and thin (Joshua 1:5; Hebrews 13:5;
Psalm 23:4)

Christ made God's will His priority (Luke 2:49)

We who are in Christ know His voice and follow His call (John 10:27-30)

Denying ungodliness we shall live righteously in this world (Titus 2:11-12)

As followers of Christ, we seek to lay aside all deceit for a brand new life
(2 Corinthians 5:15, 17)

We must deny the cravings of our sinful nature daily in order to follow the
will of God (Matthew 16:24; Romans 7:14-25)

Watch and pray because our spirit is willing to deny temptations but our
flesh is weak (Matthew 26:41)

God is always present to help us work through every situation and
circumstance we face (Psalm 46:1)

Christ is the only way to our Heavenly Father (John 14:6)

Through Christ we are no longer servants of sin (Romans 6:16-18)

The consequence of not accepting Christ as your Lord and Savior is far
worse than what we could ever imagine (Isaiah 26:20-21)

Yield yourselves unto God, as those who are alive from the dead
(Romans 6:13)

February 22—Two Birds

Those who are strong in the Lord ought to encourage the weak
(Romans 15:1)

We are not afraid because God will strengthen and uphold us with His
righteousness (Isaiah 41:10)

God's perfect will will be done in Earth as it is in Heaven (Matthew 6:10)

SPRING SECTION

March 1—What's in a Moment?

What may challenge you will only last as long as God allows it to fulfill its
purpose for spiritual growth (Genesis 50:20)

Cast all your cares on the Lord because He cares for you (1 Peter 5:7)

Our afflictions are only for a while, because what we see is only temporary
(2 Corinthians 4:17,18)

March 12—About Tithing

Tithing is a commandment of God (Leviticus 27:34) and is essentially one tenth of our increase (Numbers 18:21)

What's the Controversy? (Tithe or not)

"Christ is the end of the law for righteousness (Romans 10:4)

Tithes are a command from God (Leviticus 27:30)

God never changes (Malachi 3:6; Hebrews 13:8)

Love the Lord completely (Luke 10:27)

The law is the knowledge of sin (Romans 3:20)

Without the law we would not know right from wrong (Romans 7:7)

Sin is the transgression of the law (1 John 3:4)

The wages of sin is death (Romans 6:23a)

But the gift of God is eternal life through Christ (Romans 6:23b)

In Christ there is no sin (1 John 3:5b)

Christ freed us from the bondage of sin (Galatians 5:1)

The law of the Spirit of life in Christ Jesus set us free from the law of sin and death (Romans 8:2,4)

What we must do to be saved (John 3:5-7; Romans 10:9,10)

All Scripture is given by inspiration of God for our instruction (2 Timothy 3:16,17)

"The law is holy, . . ." The law originally served to guide actions and provide protection (Romans 7:12)

Christ did not come to destroy but to fulfill the law (Matthew 5:17)

His death, burial, and resurrection fulfilled the initial purpose of the law (Luke 19:10; 1 Corinthians 15:1-4)

We are made right through what Christ has done, not by our own actions (Ephesians 2:8,9)

Christ placed the laws upon our hearts and wrote them in our minds (Hebrews 10:16)

God will judge the secrets of humanity[3] by Jesus Christ (Romans 2:16)

Thou shalt love thy neighbor as thyself" (Matthew 22:37-39)

Two laws based on the principle of love (Romans 13:10)

When we bear one another's burdens we fulfill (follow) the law of Christ
   (Galatians 6:2)

The Lord is an advocate of order (1 Corinthians 14:40)

The Lord provides direction even into the last days (Micah 4:1-2)

Bring tithes to the storehouse (Malachi 3:10)

Consequences of not giving tithes (Malachi 3:8,9)

God warns us about pride when He mentioned how we refuse to keep his
   ordinances. "And now we call the proud happy . . ." (Malachi 3:14;15)

What Right Do We Have to Question Tithes?

God loves when we give cheerfully what we purpose in our heart
   (2 Corinthians 9:7)

Commit to what you dedicate to the Lord (Leviticus 27:10,13)

Tithes are holy unto the Lord (Leviticus 27:30)

Tithing is a personal exercise of faith (Hebrews 10:23)

Allow the Holy Spirit to guide you to the true interpretation of the
   Scriptures (John 16:13; 2 Timothy 2:15; 2 Timothy 3:16)

Get wisdom and understanding (Proverbs 4:7)

Beginning of Tithes.

The first tithe was given by Abraham (Abram) (Genesis 14:20)

References when Abraham first gave tithes (Hebrews 7:2-4)

The tithes are given as an heave offering unto the Lord (Numbers 18:20-32)

The heave offering was to be set apart, taken from the best (Exodus 29:27)

God commanded the sons of Levi to collect tithes (Hebrews 7:5)

Purpose of Tithes.

What to tithe (Deuteronomy 14:22)

A reference to the requirement of first fruits (Nehemiah 10:35 and
   Deuteronomy 18:4)

Everything we have belongs to God (Colossians 1:15-17)

When we give we are blessed to receive many benefits (Luke 6:38),
   spiritual and physical

What to do with the tithes (Deuteronomy 14:23)

Instructions for bringing tithes concerning those who were within the
   gates (Deuteronomy 14:27-29)

The Levites did not inherit any portion of the land of Canaan (Joshua 14:3; Numbers 18:23; Deuteronomy 18:1-5)

The Lord gave the Levites all the tenth for their inheritance (Numbers 18:21,24)

Food for Thought.

Tithes and offerings were brought abundantly to the house of the Lord (2 Chronicles 31:4-5,11-12)

God has a special place in His heart for the church (Ephesians 5:25b; Psalm 73:1)

Christ shall return (Matthew 24:27; 1 Thessalonians 4:16-17)

God wants us to help one another but most of all support the household of faith (Galatians 6:6-10)

"Those that be planted in the house of the Lord shall flourish in the courts of our God" (Psalm 92:13)

Why A Tenth?

God commanded a tenth of the Israelite's increase to be given to God for the descendants of Levi (Numbers 18:21,24)

The tenth shall be holy unto the Lord (Leviticus 27:30,32;)

Never add to or take away from His Word (Deuteronomy 4:2)

The Word of God will continue forever (Isaiah 40:8)

Should you start tithing or continue to tithe?

The purpose of the law originally held us accountable unto death (Deuteronomy 8:11-20)

Christ gave us a new covenant by placing the laws on our hearts and writing them in our minds (Hebrews 10:16)

You reap what you sow (Galatians 6:7)

Bring your tithes to the storehouse (the house of the Lord) (Malachi 3:10)

The Lord spoke to Jacob in a dream that revealed his future (Genesis Chapter 28:10-14)

To honor God, Jacob vowed to give a tenth of all that God gave him (Genesis 28:22)

Your spiritual development is evident by the fruit you produce (Matthew 7:20)

Final Thoughts About Tithes.

Pay your taxes but give back to God what is His (Matthew 22:15-22; Mark 12:13-17; Luke 20:20-26)

The tenth shall be holy unto the Lord (Leviticus 27:30,32;)

God takes care of the birds, He will certainly take care of you (Matthew 6:25,26)

Giving tithes is an expression of faith that God will supply all our needs (Philippians 4:19)

Without faith it is impossible to please God (Hebrews 11:6)

March 29—Why Aren't We There Yet?

Don't be anxious (Philippians 4:6)

Press towards your goal without looking back (Philippians 3:13,14)

Christ victoriously fulfilled God's plan for salvation (1 Corinthians 15:1-4)

Christ suffered and rose from the dead on the third day to pay the price for our sins (Luke 24:46)

We might forget something, cut corners, or run the other way (Jonah 1:1-3)

Complete the race that the Lord has set before you (Hebrews 12:1)

Stop trying to get ahead of God (Ecclesiastes 9:11)

God will guide you as long as you take heed to His correction (Proverbs 3:11-12)

God never fails (Zephaniah 3:5); and with God all things are possible (Matthew 19:26)

God has a plan to prosper you (Jeremiah 29:11)

All Scripture is given by inspiration of God for our instruction (2 Timothy 3:16)

Become familiar with God's Word (2 Timothy 2:15)

April 2—While We Wait

The Lord gives grace and will not withhold from them that walk uprightly (Psalm 84:11)

The Lord provided written instructions (Exodus 24:12)

Christ promised to return (Matthew 16:27,28; 2 Peter 3:12,13)

The Lord knows us personally (Luke 12:7a)

God is under complete control (Psalm 103:19)

Don't be foolish, wise in your own ways (Proverbs 26:12)

The Lord wants all to be saved (1 Timothy 2:3,4)

Watch out for the adversary (Satan) seeks to destroy (1 Peter 5:8)

Stand firm on God's Word (Ephesians 6:14; 2 Thessalonians 2:15)

Have faith in God (Mark 11:22)

Stay focused and be a light for others in the absence of the Lord until He
returns (Philippians 2:12-15)

April 6—Together As One

Christ loves the church as husbands are to love their wives (Ephesians 5:25-27)

God's chosen people (Deuteronomy 7:6-9)

God's love never fails (1 Corinthians 13:8)

The church represent Christ as the light of the world (Matthew 5:14)

Lift your hands up and bless the Lord (Psalm 134:2)

He was raised from the dead (Romans 10:9-10)

The unsaved7 are blinded by the god of this world (2 Corinthians 4:4)

The church is the pillar and ground of the truth (1 Timothy 3:15)

The church is a place where individuals gather to worship and praise God
(Psalm 35:18)

The people of God are brothers and sisters in Christ (Philippians 1:27b, 3:16b)

Vertical relationship with God through Christ (1 Timothy 2:5)

Horizontal relationship with others (Hebrews 2:11)

We are collectively committed to the same cause (Philippians 1:27b)

We must function together as one (Philippians 2:2)

What God intended for the church (Acts 17:22-34)

We represent Christ wherever we go (2 Corinthians 5:20)

All have sinned (Romans 3:23; Ephesians 6:12,13; Matthew 5:48)

As the unified body of believers in Christ we are God's dwelling place—the
temple of God (1 Corinthians 3:16)

Take care of your body which belongs to God (1 Corinthians 6:19)

It is vain not to allow your body enough rest (Psalm 127:2)

Whatever we do in word or deed; do all in the name of the Lord
(Colossians 3:17)

We are examples for others (1 Thessalonians 1:6,7; 1 Timothy 4:12)

God's Word will accomplish its purpose (Isaiah 55:11)

the body of Christ (1 Corinthians 12:27-31, Ephesians 1:23)

Christ will return for the unified body of believers (Matthew 24:27; 1
Thessalonians 4:16,17)

We are laborers together with God (1 Corinthians 3:9a)

Together we are inhabited by God through the Holy Spirit (Ephesians 2:21,22)

Love others unconditionally (John 13:34,35)

Christ loves the church (Ephesians 5:25b)

Though we are many members, we are one body in Christ (Romans 12:4,5)

Edify the body of Christ (1 Corinthians 12:12,27,28)

Where there is no vision the people perish (Proverbs 29:18)

Every member of the church has a specific calling that supports the entire
body of the church (Ephesians 4:4,11-13,22,24,32)

Receive the invitation, the call of the Lord (Revelation 3:20; Matthew 11:28;
John 7:37)

Accept salvation (Romans 10:9,10)

In the presence of the Lord (Psalm 107:8,32)

The Lord gives us strength to accomplish what we desire
(Deuteronomy 8:17,18)

The saved are strengthened (Psalm 73:26)

The eyes of the unsaved are opened (Psalm 119:18)

Edify one another (Romans 14:18,19; 1 Thessalonians 5:11)

Babe in Christ (1 Peter 2:2)

Walk in the life God intended (Corinthians 3:1-3)

We are the salt of the Earth, the flavor (Matthew 5:13)

The Lord is a shield unto them that put their trust in him (Proverbs 30:5)

God speaks to us in many ways (Jeremiah 3:15; Isaiah 52:7; Proverbs 11:30)

Faith cometh by hearing, and hearing by the word of God
(Romans 10:15,17)

Paul was appointed by God to preach to the Gentiles (Acts 9:1-20; 13:9)

Paul was given the grace to preach (Ephesians 3:8-9)

Peter's sermon in (Acts 2:34-41)

And the Lord added to the church daily such as should be saved
(Acts 2:44, 46-47)

So the Word of God may be fulfilled (Luke 4:14-21)

Praise the Lord in the assembly of the congregation (Psalm 111:1).

Exalt the Lord in the congregation and praise Him in the assembly of the
elders (Psalm 107:32)

Christ is the head over all things to the church (Ephesians 1:22)

Women in the church (1 Corinthians 14:34-35)

The Holy Spirit directs us into all truth (John 16:13)

Be not wise in your own conceits [proud notions]" (Romans 12:16)

Women were present when Jesus fed and taught the multitudes (Matthew
14:13-21; Mark 6:30-44).

Jesus commended Mary for prioritizing His teachings (Luke 10:38-42)

Christ spoke publicly with women, which was prohibited in Biblical times
(Matthew 9:20-22; Matthew 15:22)

The Good News of Jesus Christ (Matthew 28:10)

Opposing women in the church (1 Corinthians 14:34-35)

When women were expected to stay silent in the church (Timothy 2:12)

Priscilla and Aquila accompanied Paul during His ministry (Acts 18:18)

Priscilla and Aquila taught Paul salvation (Acts 18:24-26)

Women Paul highly recommended for service in the church (Romans 16:1-4)

Priscilla and Aquila had a viable ministry in their home (Romans 16:5)

Mary's support in the ministry (Romans 16:6)

The office of the bishop in (1 Timothy 3:5)

Never restrict or reject the gifts of the Holy Spirit (1 Thessalonians 5:19)

Unity for the goodness of the Lord (Jeremiah 31:11-12)

No one comes to the Father except through Christ (John 14:6)

Through the grace of God we are saved (Ephesians 2:8,9)

Not by our works, and not by church membership (Romans 10:9)

God loves us so much that He gave His only Son so we may have eternal life
(John 3:16)

God never fails (1 Chronicles 28:20b; Zephaniah 3:5)

Do what is pleasing to God (Hebrews 11:6)

The church is God's spiritual house (1 Peter 2:5)

Christ is the greatest of the house of God (1 Peter 2:6-8)

God's marvelous light (1 Peter 2:9)

God extended His grace to the entire world (1 John 2:1,2)

Those who are planted (committed to serve) in the house of the Lord will
flourish (Psalm 92:13)

Praise and bless God in the temple (Luke 24:52,53)

April 7—God Answers Prayer

God is our refuge and strength, help in times of trouble (Psalm 46:1)

In Christ we have peace because He has overcome the world (John 16:33)

I can do all things through Christ who strengthens me (Philippians 4:13)

Edify[2] one another (1 Thessalonians 5:11)

A soft answer turns away wrath, but grievance words stir up anger
(Proverbs 15:1)

Do all that you do whole-heartedly unto the Lord (Colossians 3:23)

Pray without ceasing (1 Thessalonians 5:17)

With God all things are possible (Matthew 19:26; Mark 10:27; Luke 18:27)

The Lord delivers you from all your fears (Psalm 34:4)

God answers prayer (Matthew 7:7; Mark 11:24; Luke 11:9)

Holy Spirit will give you peace (John 14:26,27)

God is greater (Deuteronomy 4:39)

Stay calm and don't worry. If you believe in God, believe in Christ
(John 14:1)

God has a plan to prosper you (Jeremiah 29:11)

The Lord will show you great and mighty things when you call on Him
(Jeremiah 33:3)

April 9—When God Calls, Listen

Know God Lord and Savior Jesus Christ (John 1:1,14; John 7:28,29)

We know when God is calling. Follow. (John 10:27)

The encouraging story of David and Goliath (1 Samuel 17)

Your season of victory will arrive, as did David's who was anointed King of
Judah (2 Samuel 2:1-7)

Never go into battle with someone else's armor (1 Samuel 17:38-39)

God will bless you even greater than you expected (2 Corinthians 10:3-5)

The Lord brought you out before, He will deliver you again.
(1 Samuel 17:37)

We can do all things through Christ who strengthens us (Philippians 4:13)

God's Word is a lamp unto your feet and a light unto your path
(Psalm 119:105)

Be glad, the Lord has overcome the world (John 16:33)

April 10—There's Something About Water

There is hope (Job 14:7-9).

Regardless of all that is going on around you, God is in the midst to help
(Psalm 46:3-5)

"In the beginning God created the heaven and the earth" (Genesis 1:1)

"And the Spirit of God moved upon the face of the waters" (Genesis 1:2b)

Come and take the water of life freely (Revelation 22:17)

Noah and his family survived a fatal worldwide flood
(Genesis Chapter 6—Chapter 9:17).

Miracle at the Red Sea (Exodus 14:21).

Miracle at the Jordan River (Joshua 3:15-17)

Christ healed a lame man at the pool of Bethesda (John 5:1-9)

Christ healed a blind man at the pool of Siloam (John Chapter 9)

Even our tears can contribute to the healing of our sorrows (2 Kings 20:5)

Peter walked on water (Matthew 14:22-33)

Peter, one of the disciples, got out of the ship and walked on water towards
Jesus (Matthew 14:28,29)

A Samaritan women learned of the living water and truth (John 4:7-29)

Rebecca met Abraham's chief servant at the well (Genesis Chapter 24)

Jesus Christ suffered for sins He did not commit (1 Peter 2:21-24).

Jesus' was rejected and wounded for our transgressions (Isaiah 53:3-5)

Water and blood came from Jesus' dead body when soldiers pierced Him in
the side (John 19:34)

The power of the Almighty God was confirmed through water which
signifies life (John 7:37-38)

The power of the Almighty God was also confirmed through Jesus' blood
which signifies death (Philippians 2:8; Isaiah 53:5)

Jesus Christ is the only Son of the true and living God
(Hebrews Chapter 1; 1 Thessalonians 1:9)

Baptism by the Holy Spirit (Mark 1:8; John 1:30-33)

We are baptized into Christ and He is within us (Galatians 3:26, 27)

April 13—What Do You See?

Peter walked on water (Matthew 14:22-33)

Incredible acts of faith (Hebrews Chapter 11)

With God all things are possible (Matthew 19:26)

No one has seen God (John 1:18; 1 John 4:12)

We will do even greater things (John 14:12)

With God all things are possible (Matthew 19:26)

May 3—Follow God's Perfect Plan

God's plan prevails (Isaiah 55:11)

Watch and pray, so not to fall into temptation (Mark 14:38)

Don't grow wearying in doing good (Galatians 6:9)

Adam and Eve sinned against God (Genesis Chapter 3)

We are justified through Christ (Romans 5:1, Galatians 3:26)

Saved by the grace of God (Ephesians 2:8)

Christ is the only capable of making the sacrifice for salvation (Acts 4:12).

God has given us a specific purpose (Ephesians 2:10)

Through Christ we can accomplish what God calls us to do (John 14:6)

The spirit is willing but the flesh is weak (Matthew 26:41)

God's grace is sufficient to develop us (2 Corinthians 12:9)

Christ came to do God's will (John 6:38)

May 14—Praise the Lord

God will cause righteousness and praise to spring forth (Isaiah 61:11)

Do not worry or be anxious for anything (Philippians 4:6)

The Lord will raise us up in due time (1 Peter 5:6, 7)

Everyone praise the Lord (Psalm 117)

Praise the Lord and be blessed (Psalm 67:5, 6)

The Lord will be praised, whether you praise Him or not (Luke 19:40)

Honor the Lord (Proverbs 3:9; Colossians 3:17)

We are here on Earth for only a short while (1 Chronicles 29:15)

Love God with all your heart (Mark 12:30)

Love others, as you love yourself (Mark 12:31)

Serve God with gladness (Psalm 100:2)

Serve others (Galatians 6:10)

Pray to God and know that He hears you and loves you forever (John 3:16)

Take time to listen to others when they are in need (Romans 12:10)

Give by faith (2 Corinthians 9:6, 7)

Demonstrate confidence in the Lord when no one else will (Luke 19:40)

Have mercy and give grace instead of casting guilt or blame (Matthew 5:7)

Don't be so quick to offend or anger (Ecclesiastes 8:9)

Apologize (Matthew 5:23, 24)

Forgive (Ephesians 4:32)

God's unfailing love and promises (2 Peter 1:4; Titus 1:2)

The Lord is worthy of praise (Psalm 24)

May 18—Action Speaks Louder with the Word

Be a doer of the Word not just a hearer (James 1:22)

See your situation in the light of truth (John 16:13)

Sometimes results from your efforts take longer than expected (Genesis Chapters 6-7)

Sometimes you'll have to step out of your comfort zone (Numbers Chapter 13)

Sometimes you're destined to go in a direction to which you are not accustomed (The Book of Esther)

Use the resources God provides. Don't hid your talents (Matthew 25:14-30)

Sometimes we have to press forward towards the goal (Philippians 4:6,7)

There is a time for everything (Ecclesiastes 3;1)

Approach God with confidence in Him (Hebrews 4:16)

With faith, we can move mountains (Matthew 21:21)

May 21—Blog Bites

We are wonderfully created by God (Psalm 139:14)

God gives us strength and perfects us (Psalm 18:32)

Everyone has the gift of hospitality (1 Peter 4:8-10)

Your priority should be set on the things of God not the things on Earth (Colossians 3:2)

Your heart is where you seek your treasures, in heaven or on Earth (Matthew 6:19-21)

Wages of sin death but salvation is a gift of life Christ Jesus (Romans 6:23)

The Lord desires that all will be saved and will come unto the knowledge of the truth (1 Timothy 2:3,4)

In Christ there is rest from our heavy burdens (Matthew 11:28-30).

God's perspective (Romans 12:3,9-21)

Trials of life are expected (1 Peter 4:12,13)

Christ has overcome the world (John 16:33)

Forgive others because we are forgiven (Matthew 6:14)

The Lord forgives us (Colossians 3:12,13)

God will punish those who do evil against you (Romans 12:19)

Tomorrow is not promised (Romans 13:10-11; Proverbs 27:1)

Let go of what is keeping you from moving forward, forgiving, loving, achieving (Philippians 3:13,14)

What pleases God: do justly, love mercy, walk humbly (Micah 6:8; 1 Thessalonians 4:1-12)

Be still (Psalm 46:10)

Attitude of a righteous parent (Ephesians 6:4; Psalm 127:3,4)

Everything that happens has a purpose and works out for good (Romans 8:28)

God is Great! (Psalm 48:1; 86:10; 95:3; 145:3)

God can do anything because He created everything (Colossians 1:16; John 1:3; Romans 11:36)

Nothing is too hard for God (Jeremiah 32:17)

God hears our prayers (1 John 5:14, 15)

God always keeps His promises (Hebrews 10:23; Zephaniah 3:5)

All Scripture is given by inspiration of God for instruction in righteousness for our perfection (2 Timothy 3:16,17)

God's plan for our lives is greater than we realize (Jeremiah 29:11)

As far as we can see is not as far as we can go in life (Isaiah 55:9)

By faith, we can accomplish what God has purposed (Hebrews 11:1)

God's purpose will be fulfilled (Isaiah 55:10,11)

The world will pass away but those that abide in God will last forever (1 John 2:17)

Those who follow God's plan move forward and receive the blessings He promised (2 Corinthians 1:20)

Take the first step of faith (Luke 17:5,6)

Look to Christ (Hebrews 12:2)

When we explore the entire Word of God we open our hearts to God's new mercies (Psalm 87:1-3)

God never changes (James 1:17)

God has a plan to prosper you (Jeremiah 29:11)

God provides some of the desires of your heart when He is the center of your life (Psalm 37:4)

May 30—Able to Stand

Not knowing the Scriptures is a mistake (Matthew 22:29)

The Holy Spirit dwells within us (2 Timothy 1:14)

Prepare to stand up against the uncertainties of life (Ephesians 6:13-17)

Study and retain the Word in your mind and in your heart (Psalm 119:11)

God will do everything He said He will (Isaiah 46:9-10; 11)

God will keep us from falling (Jude 1:24,25)

God is always with us (Isaiah 43:5)

God promised to strengthen and keep us (2 Thessalonians 3:3)

God is greater (1 John 4:4)

Stand in total faith (Hebrews 11:1)

God knows our capabilities because our strength is in Him (Colossians 1:10,11)

Stand the tests of life for our good (Philippians 1:6)

Stand the tests of life for God's glory (Isaiah 43:7)

"Every day brings
new experiences that sometimes
challenge our expectations
while preparing us
for days to come"
~~*Genia*